LITERARY CELEBRITY IN CANADA

LORRAINE YORK

Literary Celebrity in Canada

UNIVERSITY OF TORONTO PRESS
Toronto Buffalo London

© University of Toronto Press Incorporated 2007
Toronto Buffalo London
Printed in Canada

ISBN 978-0-8020-9282-3

Printed on acid-free paper

Library and Archives Canada Cataloguing in Publication

York, Lorraine M. (Lorraine Mary), 1958–
Literary celebrity in Canada / Lorraine York.

Includes bibliographical references and index.
ISBN 978-0-8020-9282-3

1. Authorship – Social aspects – Canada – History – 20th century.
2. Authors, Canadian (English) – 20th century – Biography.
3. Celebrities – Canada – Biography.   4. Authors and readers –
Canada – History – 20th century.   5. Literature and society –
Canada – History – 20th century.   I. Title.

PS8061.Y67 2007   C810.9′005   C2007-901359-7

University of Toronto Press acknowledges the financial assistance to
its publishing program of the Canada Council for the Arts and the
Ontario Arts Council.

This book has been published with the help of a grant from the
Canadian Federation for the Humanities and Social Sciences,
through the Aid to Scholarly Publications Programme, using funds
provided by the Social Sciences and Humanities Research Council
of Canada.

University of Toronto Press acknowledges the financial support for
its publishing activities of the Government of Canada throught he
Book Publishing Industry Development Program (BPIDP).

Contents

Acknowledgments

I have been the beneficiary of so many people's expertise, advice, good will, and patience from the very beginning of this project. Many thanks to Melanie Holmes, working on a Student Assistantship Bursary at McMaster, for doing the start-up research that allowed me to apply for a SSHRC Standard Research Grant, and to anonymous colleagues who thought the project was deserving of SSHRC support. Because of that support, I was blessed with the most generous and hard-working research assistant one could ever ask for: Kate Higginson. The broad spectrum of sources, from scholarly book to newspaper to internet, drawn upon in this book appears thanks to Kate's meticulous work. Kate: thank you; I always said the trick would be to produce a book worthy of your contributions.

Colleagues and friends have been kind and generous in their support of this project: Sarah Brophy, the soul of collegiality, emailed me source information on Australian fame; Robert Lecker and the people at *Essays on Canadian Writing* let me meander on about this topic in its very early stages in their twentieth-anniversary issue. The chairs of my department of English and cultural studies, first Don Goellnicht and now Mary O'Connor, have been unstinting in their support for all of the research of department memebers. Thanks to Neil McLaughlin, Department of Sociology at McMaster, for reading sections of the manuscript and offering perceptive feedback. Colleagues Daniel Coleman, Ron Granofsky, Grace Kehler, and Peter

Walmsley inspire me; they are a delight to work with and learn from. So are the graduate students I have had the honour to teach in Celebrity/Culture for the past three years: Nick Buffo, Heather Colpitts, Brady Curlew, Karen Espiritu, Andrew Griffin, Mandy Koolen, Dana Woloschuk, Katrine Raymond, Suzanne Rintoul, Jana Roloson, Lesley Steeve, Scott Stoneman, Bonnie Wong, Robin Chamberlain, Liz Harmer, Wafa Hasan, Paul Huebener, Krista Lively, Dilia Narduzzi, Christy O'Connor, Jason Phillips, Kevin Pighin, Colleen Court, Jeremy Sullivan, Jillaine Tuininga, Jessica Carey, Meagan Dallimore, Liat Dobrishman, William Edwards, Sarah Henderson, Amanda Lim, Jody McNabb, Michael Mikulak, Alexis Muirhead, Robbie Richardson, Rebecca Ross, and Delora Skelton. What amazing people.

At University of Toronto Press, Siobhan McMenemy has been, as usual, a wonderful editor to work with. I submitted the manuscript to UTP deliberately in hopes of having a chance to work with her again. Barbara Tessman copyedited the manuscript with care and insight, saving me from myself on many of these pages. A heartfelt thank you to those anonymous assessors who gave of their time and expertise to help me make this a better book.

Deepest appreciation goes to my family: my siblings Reg York, Peggy Frank, Marie Thody, and Pat Homenuck; my partner, Michael Ross, who supports, encourages, critiques, and cheers me on with irrepressible energy and wit; and my daughter, Anna Ross, who works so very hard at everything she does and yet is the most sociable person I know. You are my role model!

LITERARY CELEBRITY IN CANADA

1 Literary Celebrity?

Authors have, in one sense, never been more visible in Canada than they have in recent decades. Literary festivals and readings attract growing numbers of listeners, large book chains such as Chapters and Indigo sponsor author appearances, and community reading clubs have become so successful that publishers often gear texts for their use, offering club-friendly 'questions for further discussion' at the end of chosen works. But in another sense, the author figure is peculiarly absent from our conception of Canadian literature. In academic circles, this is partly due to the refocusing of critical energies away from authorial intention in the wake of poststructuralist rethinkings of authorship and textuality. Authors are, popularly speaking, visible and active in the promotion of their wares in a major way, and yet critical writing on literature directs attention away from this figure, often fruitfully reframing the discussion in terms of ideology and power. This studied avoidance produces a curious disjunction between professional and more generally informed consumers of literary writing. *Literary Celebrity in Canada* seeks to address and negotiate this disjunction. It is the first full-length study of the author as media persona in Canada and it theorizes literary celebrity as it operates in – and in tension with – this national setting. That said, this book addresses the author as public persona very much in terms of ideological tension and contestation.

At the same time, *Literary Celebrity in Canada* casts doubt upon the notion of a specifically Canadian approach to fame, a notion that is surprisingly prevalent, not only in journalistic but also in academic circles. Fame is, I argue, performed in different keys by particular star authors, depending on the various sets of meanings circulating in their star image. These meanings can be contradictory, incommensurate, and complex, so it is no coincidence that one of the conditions most prevalent among the literary celebrities whom I examine in this study is uneasiness. Celebrity, after all, signals the meeting and exchange of the public and private realms, and such a condition is itself productive of uneasiness. In star authors, that uneasiness may involve the terms of the revelation of their public and private selves. How much of a self does an author, now encouraged by agents and publishers to appear in numerous public venues, feel called upon to perform? For women writers in particular, the performance may involve handling prurient curiosity about the terms of their private domestic situations; Margaret Atwood, for instance, is a canny balancer of the public and the private, but even she evolved this balance only after a period of adjustment and tension.

For other authors, particularly those born outside the country, citizenship itself becomes an uneasy condition of their celebrity; I examine, in this regard, the exoticizing of the public image of Michael Ondaatje and the different citizenship tension in the star image of the late Carol Shields, who managed a precarious balance of her own, as a Canadian citizen and winner of the prestigious Pulitzer Prize for American writers. In Shields, too, I see another sort of uneasiness, one involving the speed of celebrity. As theorist P. David Marshall has noted, the word 'celebrity' is linked etymologically to, among other meanings, speed and transience, through the Latin root 'celere' (swift) (6). Shields is a good example of the celebrated author for whom celebrity arrived late; this belatedness gives rise to another uneasy situation that also attends the phenomenon of celebrity in general, which is the need both to recognize sudden fame as a testament to talent and to temper fame's legendary swiftness with proof of cultural value, in the form of literary apprenticeships steeped over a longer period of time.

No one version of literary celebrity, therefore, fits all, and no nationally specific performance of celebrity marks Canadian literary stars. But of the many tensions that have arisen in the various ways in which authors perform their celebrity, the one that I have found appearing with remarkable consistency, in different guises, involves citizenship. For Canadian writers, this tension is exacerbated by their positioning next to the large American English-language market, what Timothy Brennan has referred to as 'a kind of corporate literary salon' (39). As Nick Mount shows in his study of early-twentieth-century Canadian émigré authors, that continental salon has long exerted a powerful pull, and many of the citizenship tensions that I examine in contemporary writers find their historical echo in the cultural double-bind faced by those earlier writers. Although he argues that the choice faced by writers in the 1890s and 1900s – to stay or to leave – wasn't about 'giving up one national literary culture for another; it was about moving from the margins to the centre of a continental literary culture' (13), the decision to leave was often figured by the home audience as a desertion of national culture. In fact, Mount argues, in the years to come, critics and writers effectively wrote these émigré writers out of literary histories of Canada or represented their work selectively, according to its degree of Canadian content. If celebrity marks the uneasy space wherein the single, special individual and the group demographic both meet and separate, then citizenship, as a condition wherein the individual and the group mutually define each other, is a prime expression of that uneasy space. *Literary Celebrity in Canada* explores that space.

At first glance, the very notion of literary celebrity may seem like a contradiction in terms. Can we really use words like 'fame' and 'celebrity' to describe writers, those notorious privacy-seeking, solitary scribblers? As historian Daniel Boorstin noted sardonically in the early 1960s, the distinguished American playwright Arthur Miller 'became a "real" celebrity by his marriage to Marilyn Monroe' (65). According to the conventional wisdom, writers cannot, it appears, be real celebrities because the proving grounds of global celebrity are not the bookstore, publishing house, or an individual reader's private experience of consuming words. They are, instead, those globalized media, such as film, television, and pop music, that draw mass audiences. Of course, this supposition assumes that there is a dominant notion of celebrity against which all other pretenders to fame must measure themselves. In this book, I rely on more sophisticated theories of celebrity, drawn from film studies and from cultural criticism, in order to analyse the workings of celebrity culture within a particular sector of cultural production: the Canadian publishing industry. How do notions of celebrity inform the way that writers are currently marketed in Canada, a nation whose geographical closeness to the United States has created a corresponding proximity to its influential popular culture? One way of considering this question is through the study of three contemporary writers who have been deemed literary stars: Margaret Atwood, Michael Ondaatje, and Carol Shields. So as not to fall into the assumption that celebrity is a purely present-day phenomenon (as cultural theorists who see celebrity as a modern debasement of heroism would have us believe), I consider the celebrity of these three authors against the historical backdrop of earlier Canadian literary renown, as represented here by the illustrious quartet of Lucy Maud Montgomery, Pauline Johnson, Stephen Leacock, and Mazo de la Roche. What has changed in Canadian literary celebrity, what has remained constant, and what do the changes herald for younger generations of up-and-coming Canadian writers?

The choice of these four earlier and three current literary stars was not as difficult as it might seem. I looked for writers whose media coverage featured a more than incidental or fleeting use of the discourse of stardom. In the case of the earlier writers, the founding and maintenance of tourist sites devoted to the writer (Montgomery and Leacock) made some choices fairly predictable. Pauline Johnson's high-profile stage career made her an obvious choice, as did Mazo de la Roche's much-publicized winning of a prestigious American literary prize. True, other early writers were recipients of prizes, but de la Roche's winning of the Atlantic Monthly Prize caused an unprecedented stir. In addition, de la Roche was significant in explicitly embracing the 'lifestyle' of literary nobility. In the case of my three choices of current literary stars, alternates could certainly be proposed, but I found, in a survey of media coverage of these three writers, a significantly larger concentration of the language of stardom. An equally obvious choice would have been Leonard Cohen, and scholars in the field might reasonably wonder at his exclusion. But his celebrity was taken to an international level through his work in the recording industry, which, in turn, fed into his literary acclaim. For my study, on specifically literary celebrity, I wanted examples of writers whose fame, no matter what Hollywoodized forms it might subsequently have assumed, derived from their labour as writers of books.

Other choices would have been equally possible, and for a time I planned to use the example of Alice Munro to provide an epilogue to the study. Munro's unquestioned celebrity – paired with her legendary reluctance, until recently, to participate in more than a minimal number of publicity events arranged by her publishers – would make, I thought, a challenging case to counterpose against those of more visible Canadian literary stars, as would Marie-Claire Blais, whom I also considered. But in Michael Ondaatje I found a suggestive example of the reclusive celebrity whose equally legendary private nature contrasted even more forcefully with his Hollywood-promoted celebrity after the success of *The English Patient*. In Quebec, there is no doubt that Michel Tremblay is a literary star, and I considered him, too, as a possible object of analysis. In terms of frequency of references to his stardom in the media, however, he did not attract quite as much comment of this sort as did my three choices. A study of Tremblay as literary celebrity would have the advantage of spanning a number of decades, like Atwood, and encompassing a number of positionings in relation to key political questions over those years, such as language and nationalism. It would be fascinating to see how those changing political conditions have affected perceptions of his celebrity.

Because of the tendency for celebrity to become a monolithic term, I want to begin by considering how celebrity has been variously defined by cultural theorists, and how my own understanding of celebrity in the literary field of production has been inflected and deflected by some of those definitions. The mid-twentieth-century social commentary of Daniel Boorstin (his influential book *The Image*) and C. Wright Mills (*The Power Elite*) took a predominantly sour view of celebrity. Boorstin proclaimed that '*The celebrity is a person who is known for his well-known-ness*' (57; emphasis in original), a spare axiom to say the least. For Boorstin, the celebrity is a hollowed-out version of an earlier age's hero; such a view entertains an ahistorical nostalgia and, as critics such as Richard Dyer have pointed out, gives no detailed insight into the processes by which people become celebrities. For Mills, the celebrity took over from the earlier cultural elites, the 'society lady and man of pedigreed wealth' (71). Like Boorstin, Mills was unremittingly critical of what he saw as the cultural emptiness of celebrities, and he, too, captured this theory of celebrity emptiness in a spare, axiomatic turn of phrase: 'Rather than being celebrated because they occupy positions of prestige, they occupy positions of prestige because they are celebrated' (74). This emptiness theory would filter directly into the much-publicized, influential theories of a next generation of cultural critics: Neil Postman in his critique of television culture, *Amusing Ourselves to Death*, and Neal Gabler in *Life, the Movie: How Entertainment Conquered Reality*, to name just two. Both of these theorists see celebrity as essentially vacuous products of manufacture.

It is far more surprising, though, to perceive the emptiness theory at work in more recent studies of celebrity, many of which openly contest the assumptions of that theory. And yet several of these recently published books betray the emptiness theory's persistent traces. Graeme Turner's *Understanding Celebrity* (2004), for example, warns that analyses such as Boorstin's are typical of 'elite critiques of movements in popular culture' wherein 'each new shift in fashion is offered as the end of civilisation as we know it, with the real motivation being an elitist distaste for the demotic or populist dimension of mass cultural

practices' (5). For his part, Turner rightly emphasizes, in concluding his study, that 'celebrity has the potential to operate in
ways that one might deplore or applaud, but neither potential is
intrinsic' (137). Still, the balance of his own commentary on
the celebrity phenomenon tends to deplore rather than to
applaud. He opens his book by noting that the fame of present-
day celebrities 'does not necessarily depend on the position or
achievements that gave them their prominence in the first
instance. Rather, ... their fame is likely to have outstripped the
claims to prominence developed within that initial location'
(3). Such an observation reads like a vintage Boorstin-style critique of the emptiness of celebrity. And the manifestations of
contemporary celebrity that Turner focuses on in the individual
chapters of *Understanding Celebrity* tend towards the deplorable
too: web sites featuring nude celebrities, the fleeting celebrity
of reality television actors, the 'DIY' (do-it-yourself) celebrity of
'cam girls' (64–8), and tabloids.

Similarly, Joshua Gamson's *Claims to Fame* both disavows and
reinstates the emptiness theory. Though he refers to Boorstin's
'take on fame' as 'persuasive' (9), he adds that a 'quieter, but
nonetheless significant, set of voices has counteracted the hand-
wringing critiques, arguing that commercial culture is not
nearly as powerful, and those consuming it not nearly as powerless, as the critics propose' (10). For his own part, he determines to let both schools of thought have their say in his book:
'It is the ambition of this book,' he declares, 'to dismiss neither
the concerns of the critics nor the pleasures and freedoms and
meanings that participants in entertainment-celebrity culture
derive' (11). But as with Turner's *Understanding Celebrity*, both
the overture and the balance of analysis of Gamson's *Claims to
Fame* undermine this worthy ambition. He opens his book with
the case study of 'Angelyne,' a woman in Hollywood who has
constructed a type of 'DIY' celebrity by posing as a 'blonde
bombshell' and letting tourists take pictures of her as souvenirs
of the capital of celluloid fame. Gamson's reflection on Angelyne's celebrity is a virtual echo of Boorstin's famous circular
axiom: 'Talent has nothing to do with it: she wants to be cele-

brated not for doing but for being' (1). Fittingly, then, his introduction to his study amounts to an apologia for taking up the
subject at all. As he explains, 'The space celebrities occupy, we
will see, is not necessarily a deep one, and the experience of it is
not necessarily weighty. The time, resources, and energy
devoted to it are all the more puzzling. Indeed, in this book the
often blatant shallowness of the entertainment celebrity arena
is taken as a starting point, and the challenge will be to mine
the superficialities for their depths' (6). Celebrity is, again, that
spare, tautological surface that Boorstin imagined it to be when
he included it in a long list of American culture's 'pseudo-
events' – appearances taken for realities, 'superficialities,' in
Gamson's terms, taken for 'depths.' And although Gamson
returns, later in the book, to his original objective of evenhand-
edness – his resolution to 'applaud' as well as 'deplore,' as
Turner would say – he remains conflicted. Though he criticizes
Charles Marowitz's Boorstinesque reflection that 'In the old
days, fame was the result of achievement' by reminding readers
that the 'link between "status" and "excellence" has never been
absolute,' still 'celebrity has become increasingly industrialized,' and, in this sense, Marowitz's 'argument hits the mark'
(40). In grounding his own analysis in a historical distinction
between the 'early' days of Hollywood celebrity and later manifestations, Gamson devises a narrative of deterioration from
value to hollow hype. He concludes his chapter on late-twenti-
eth-century fame by noting that

> the artificial-manufacture story ... offers a strange new interplay
> between hierarchy and egalitarian democracy. On the one hand,
> it brings its own radical egalitarianism: a world where attention
> will be distributed more evenly, if in shorter increments; a world
> where stardom is more accessible since the inborn requirements
> are fewer; a world in which anyone who can lip-synch can feel the
> glow of celebrity. On the other hand, it celebrates (even as it
> attacks) a new, powerful elite: the media, the industry, the star
> makers, able to make and control images, able to direct mass
> attention through marketing machinery. (54)

Gamson's formulations – on the one hand / on the other hand, his use of comparatives ('more evenly,' 'shorter,' 'more accessible,' 'fewer') – reveal both this passage's conflicted nature and its inclination towards a theory of empty value and soulless manufacture.

While it may, indeed, sometimes be the case that celebrity is vacuous, unearned, or manufactured, I nevertheless prefer a definition of celebrity that at least holds open the possibility that being celebrated need not always be a negative thing, that it can operate and signify variously within culture, and that audiences, in turn, can act and signify upon it. For such a definition, I turned to film studies, though, as film critics such as Richard Dyer and Richard deCordova commented as relatively recently as 1990, previous work on stars and celebrities that emerged from film studies tends to be anecdotal and untheorized. Starting in 1979 with Dyer's own *Stars*, a more rigorous study of stars took its place. One definition of stardom that issues from film studies and that manages to avoid the inherent negativity of the Mills–Boorstin–inspired school, is, simply, that celebrity signals the growing importance of narratives of the personal life of the film actor, to the point that the life story becomes of equal importance to the actor's performances. DeCordova makes exactly this point when he distinguishes between picture personalities and stars; whereas 'knowledge about the picture personality,' who, according to deCordova, emerged around 1909, 'was restricted to the player's professional existence,' 'the star is characterized by a fairly thoroughgoing articulation of the paradigm professional / private life,' and so 'the question of the player's existence outside his/her work in films entered discourse' (deCordova in Gledhill 25–6). DeCordova is largely non-judgmental about this transition, whereas Neal Gabler, working in the tradition of Boorstin, is deeply critical of what he calls the 'lifie' or 'life movie,' the process by which the importance of the artist's own life supersedes that of the artistic product (128). Film critics tend to be accepting of the notion of the lifie, perhaps because they perceive a porous boundary between star persona and star performance;

at any rate, film and television critic John Ellis defines stardom as 'lifie' in a way that proves particularly fruitful for my study of literary production: 'The basic definition of a star is that of a performer in a particular medium whose figure enters into subsidiary forms of circulation, and then feeds back into future performances' (91). This is exactly what I wish to study and assess in Canadian literary publishing: what happens when a performer in a particular medium – words – enters into what Ellis calls 'subsidiary forms of circulation': for my purposes, advertising, television and radio interviews, magazine profiles, book launches, the hiring of agents, prize competitions, and other commercial activities.

The other sort of definition of celebrity that I was searching for, of celebrity as operating variously within culture, is to be found in the ideological approaches to celebrity that arose largely out of the work of Richard Dyer. As Christine Gledhill notes, Dyer introduced the notion of a 'star text' – the idea that the 'star' is, in Gledhill's words, 'an intertextual construct produced across a range of media and cultural practices' (xiv). For Dyer, star texts do ideological work of a complex kind: 'star images function crucially in relation to contradictions within and between ideologies, which they seek variously to "manage" or resolve' (Stars 38). One of those contradictions regularly mentioned by people writing on celebrity is the one between privacy or intimacy and publicity; though stars appear to be above the ordinary, in a privileged realm of their own that is inaccessible to the fan, fans also assume that they have a right to know everything about the celebrity, to dissect the most personal of their tics and choices. How much more heightened that contradiction between privacy and publicity appears in the specific case of literary celebrities. As I mentioned at the opening of this chapter, it seems anomalous even to consider a cultural job that is, in this culture at least, most frequently performed in privacy as a likely basis for the sort of publicity-driven celebrity that is so pervasive today. The very activity that has given rise to the writer's well-knownness – writing – is exactly that which cannot be represented to advantage in the primarily visual marketing media: television, for example. Documentary filmmakers dealing with writers most often content themselves with fleeting images of the writer seated at a desk or in front of a computer. And, ironically, the never-ending round of public readings, book signings, and launches that are the expected staple of the aspiring and successful author alike take that author away from what he or she would no doubt prefer and need to be doing at that moment: writing, alone. In my view, literary celebrity seeks, in Dyer's words, to 'manage or resolve' this tension between the writer as a public and a private agent in some way, though the fault lines remain very much in evidence.

Recent, emerging work on literary celebrity tends to emphasize the irony of this situation. Joe Moran, for instance, sees literary celebrity as a paradoxical mixture of seeming 'aloofness' from the commercial crossroads and participation in that realm of commodities; the literary star, in his words, embodies a 'nostalgia for some kind of transcendent, anti-economic, creative element in a secular, debased, commercialized culture' (9). Very recent work in this rapidly developing field tends to gravitate towards modernist writers, probably because the ironies of privacy and publicity, of the world of texts and the world of marketing, are most dramatic in this period and aesthetic; Loren Glass, in *Authors Inc.: Literary Celebrity in the Modern United States, 1880–1980*, wryly notes, for instance, that 'few things are more striking about the primary spokespeople for modernism than the contrast between their stated theories of self-effacement and their actual practice and literary-historical destiny of self-aggrandizement and even shameless self-promotion' (5). In *Modernism and the Culture of Celebrity*, Aaron Jaffe agrees that 'prominent modernists – Eliot, Pound, Joyce, Lewis ... – were more canny about fashioning their careers – indeed, fashioning the very notion of a literary career – than is often appreciated' (3). He refers to this complex positioning of modernist writers vis-à-vis celebrity as 'a stance of ironic accommodation' (176–7).

Such studies as Moran's, Glass's, and Jaffe's productively read the ideological ironies of the very concept of literary celebrity.

Building on the work of Dyer, and of Foucault, Richard deCordova takes ideological critique of filmic celebrity in another direction: towards the celebrity system as a site for constructing social knowledge of sexuality. Referring to the seemingly insatiable public appetite for details about stars' private lives, deCordova argues that 'the very modes of knowing the star, of investigating the truth of his or her identity, are linked to and a part of a broader strategy of deploying sexuality in modern times' (*Picture Personalities* 141). Following Foucault, deCordova sees the star system as a type of social confessional, a site where 'the sexual stands as the privileged, ultimate truth of the private' (142–3). In some cases of literary celebrity I discern a similarly sexualized desire for details of authors' private lives, particularly where authors are socially marked, for whatever reason, as exotic or transgressive.

Whether ideological readings of stardom address sexuality or contradictions between notions of privacy and publicity, they are all, in some way or other, concerned with the question of celebrity and power. In fact, the question of what sort of power, exactly, celebrities possess has been a moot point in writings about stardom for some years. In many earlier works, critics assume that stars, although they wield a seductive appeal, do not possess power as such. As P. David Marshall has pointed out, in the early 1970s the Italian sociologist Francesco Alberoni provided 'one of the first interpretations of celebrities in terms of a concept of power' (15), though he ultimately saw that power as non-institutional in nature, more along the lines of cultural influence. The title of Alberoni's influential essay on celebrity, 'The Powerless Elite,' deliberately rebutted C. Wright Mills's notion of celebrity as an extension or modernization of older economic and social 'power elites.' Such an analysis could have been written only before the American presidency of Ronald Reagan.

In Marshall's book, *Celebrity and Power: Fame in Contemporary Culture*, the question of the nature of celebrity power gets the sustained theoretical treatment that it requires. With a nod to Alberoni, Marshall does acknowledge that, for the most part, celebrities 'are not powerful in any overt political sense,' but they do articulate systems of cultural power, particularly those involving concepts of individuality and collectivity. 'The celebrity,' writes Marshall, 'is a negotiated "terrain" of significance. To a great degree, the celebrity is a production of the dominant culture ...: Nevertheless, the celebrity's meaning is constructed by the audience. An exact "ideological fit" between production of the cultural icon and consumption is rare. Audience members actively work on the presentation of the celebrity in order to make it fit into their everyday experiences' (or, I'd add, sometimes, *not* to fit) (47). The point is similar to that made by Richard Dyer in *Stars*; there, he emphasizes his preference for a theory of celebrity that neither overemphasizes stardom as a creation of production or of consumption, as he feels most theories have done to date (emptiness theories, for example, which emphasize top-down hegemonic production of stars, and psychoanalysis, which stresses the consumption of stars through audience projection, dream work, and the like). Instead, he argues, 'production and consumption are differentially determining forces in the creation of stars (producers always having more power over commodities than consumers), but both are always mediated by and in ideology' (20).

An ideological approach to celebrity power has many implications for a study of literary celebrity. First of all, it provides one way of handling the common assumption that I mentioned at the beginning: the idea that writers do not have sufficient social or economic power for them to be considered stars. Writers, too, are what Marshall would call negotiated terrains of social significance, and their production and consumption reveal a veritable struggle for cultural authority. Those who are given special, elevated status as literary celebrities are given extra latitude to speak and to be listened to. As the cultural theorist Pierre Bourdieu put it, 'The struggle in the field of cultural production over the imposition of the legitimate mode of cultural production is inseparable from the struggle within the dominant class ... to impose the dominant principle of domination (that is to say – ultimately – the definition of human accomplishment)' (41).

If the struggle to claim and bestow celebrity is, as Bourdieu says, nothing less than a struggle over what gets defined as human accomplishment, then celebrity is fully implicated in theoretical discussions about subjectivity itself. In recent ideological approaches to celebrity, like those of Bourdieu, Dyer, and Marshall, what I find particularly valuable is the way in which celebrity, with its attendant discourses of authenticity or inauthenticity, is crucially related to the social and historical construction of the self. In some ways, this is not a new thought; in 1960 Edgar Morin wrote that the star 'proposes and imposes a new ethics of individuality, which is that of modern leisure' (177), though his main preoccupation in his book *The Stars* was with how celebrity forms a cult or religion for acolyte-fans in a predominantly secular world. Still, Morin planted the idea that to be a star was to model a particularly modern form of being an individual.

Stacey Margolis takes a closer look at the modernization of the self in celebrity, taking as her point of departure a study of the figures of celebrities in Edith Wharton's fiction and the status of celebrity privacy in the legal discourse of the time. She notes that, in Wharton's fiction, 'rather than making one's claim to the self stronger by increasing its value, publicity actually seems to dissolve all claims to the self as a private property' (89). Margolis cites contemporary legal decisions to the same effect; before the 1950s, celebrities had a very difficult time proving that their image could be appropriated or used inappropriately, since the prevailing assumption was that they had allowed their image to become public property and so had ceded private property rights. Margolis cites one case where a famous football player protested against a company using his photograph to sell calendars; his protests were disregarded by the courts. Ironically, under this legal dispensation, celebrities do not, as we generally think of them today, transform themselves successfully into valuable pieces of public property. Rather, they *fail*, in Margolis's words, 'to successfully transform the self into private property' (90)

The stage is now set for twentieth-century celebrity, which

rises, phoenix-like, out of the ashes of previous discourses of the private self. If celebrities are forced to see themselves as commodities in a market rather than as private persons holding defensible privacy rights, then the only route left to protect themselves is by extending commodity ownership rights over the most private-seeming of personal attributes. This is exactly what happened over the course of the twentieth century. Jane M. Gaines, in her book *Contested Culture*, traces the evolution of publicity rights out of the right-to-privacy doctrine that arose in the United States; according to these rights, as Gaines says, 'a celebrity can claim a "personal monopoly" in his or her image' (186). Considered from this perspective, the recent cases of singer-actresses Jennifer Lopez and Mariah Carey reportedly insuring body parts (derrière and legs respectively) for a considerable sum are only a bizarre recent chapter in the legal history of celebrity in North America. Even unauthorized use of an image related to the star can be considered a violation of a property right. Gaines cites the case of Jacqueline Kennedy Onassis suing the Dior company for the use of her image in one of their magazine advertisements. The image was not strictly one of Onassis, however; it was a photograph of a model who looked uncannily like her. This was enough, though, to constitute a violation of Onasssis's publicity rights. As Gaines notes of the philosophical confusions surrounding such a decision, 'privacy doctrine and the publicity right that has evolved out of it (as they have dealt with issues regarding celebrity images), depend on an unexamined assumption that the unauthorized use of a photograph is an appropriation of the identity of the person photographed' (86) – even when the person actually being photographed is not the celebrity in question but a simulacrum.

Margolis is right, therefore, to observe that what was being debated in twentieth-century celebrity legal cases was nothing less than the 'phenomenological problem of the self in modernity' (89). It is left to P. David Marshall, in his study of celebrity and power, to draw out the ideological consequences of this phenomenological debate about privacy, publicity, and the celebrity self: 'The celebrity as public individual who participates openly as a marketable commodity serves as a powerful type of legitimation of the political economic model of exchange and value – the basis of capitalism – and extends that model to include the individual' (x).

One of the most enduring legacies of this legal and philosophical debate over the privacy and publicity of celebrity selves is the unstable relationship between celebrity and notions of authenticity and inauthenticity. Writings about celebrity – from the academic treatise to the most recent scandal sheet on the grocery store shelves – are filled with the question of what constitutes the reality or the real life of the stars, if such a thing can even be conceptualized. In his article 'A Star Is Born and the Construction of Authenticity,' Richard Dyer zeroes in on a central paradox of celebrity. As Dyer points out, the question of authenticity is closely related to the rise of modern conceptions of humanism and individualism because once the performer or self is seen as an agent of social action, then the whole question of whether he or she is performing truthfully is of crucial importance. But herein lies the paradox: we live in an age where there is widespread acceptance of the idea that stars are made, constructed, rather than born, so how can a belief in a manufacture thesis of celebrity sit comfortably alongside a belief in stars' authenticity as stars? Dyer says it can, and he suggests some philosophical reasons why it often does. For example, the star inhabits a person who we know does, in some way, conduct a life away from public scrutiny, in however difficult a fashion, and Dyer says that the fact that we know or sense this tempts us to read stars as both 'made' and 'authentic' (135). Earlier in Hollywood, Dyer writes, there was great pressure to keep all representations of a star looking consistent, and there was also a great deal of pressure on stars not to act publicly in ways that were blatantly inconsistent with their star personas. Though this pressure still obtains today, it operates more in the sector of commercial endorsements, for stars must still keep some minimal vigilance over the compatibility of their image with that of the product they are promoting (McCracken). But otherwise, in the wake of major scandals in the Hollywood of the 1920s, this pressure has dissipated greatly. Still, as Dyer points out, authenticity remains a very unstable, tricky force in celebrity culture. For example, if a production company or agent goes to great lengths to produce an image of the star exactly as he or she appears in films, the public is likely to rebel and label the image inauthentic and contrived. Also to be considered are the variable of time and the datedness of signs of authenticity; as Dyer wryly notes, 'yesterday's markers of sincerity and authenticity are today's signs of hype and artifice' (137). A quick glance at 1950s television commercials should offer a case in point.

   All of these celebrity phenomena – the construction of a self in modernity, the paradox of star manufacture and star authenticity, the instability of celebrity authenticity – seem, at first glance, to have relevance mainly to the stars of film, television, and popular music. Certainly, in scholarly treatments of these phenomena, film stars are most often used to exemplify them. But they register just as strongly in the careers of writers, who, since the nineteenth century, have been sought after for interviews and special commentary or insight into their work. One of the earliest North American literary star personaes to receive this treatment, Mark Twain, once complained that 'if papers and magazines can get and print interviews with me ... they won't buy my articles, and then where should I be?' (1357). Which self should I be marketing, Twain seems to be asking – the persona of my articles or the persona of myself as an author being interviewed? Writers of the past couple of centuries have been increasingly caught up in this dilemma. More and more, they need to be visible, promoting their books and meeting their readership, and yet the more they do this, the more they present before their readers' eyes a self that, like the celebrities of the early twentieth century, they might prefer to keep private and uncommodified. At a time, too, when writers increasingly resist the idea that the representations of persons they create – on the stage or in the pages of a novel – are not to be confused, in a naive autobiographical reading, with themselves, this increasingly public presence as media personalities tends to confirm the link between the writer and the book in the public mind. Faced with these pressures, in what ways do authors in Canada today perform their writing selves? And what are the implications of their increasingly public performances?

Many cultural critics have glanced at the phenomenon of literary celebrity, usually in the context of their main focus on visual media personalities, but their conclusions about that seemingly anomalous breed, the literary celebrity, are as varied as their theoretical positions on celebrity itself. The Boorstin tradition of celebrity critique sees literary celebrity as yet another sign of decline from a formerly Edenic state of literate good taste and high standards. In *The Image* Daniel Boorstin critiques what he sees as the domination of the American literary scene by 'a few stars – Ernest Hemingway, Norman Mailer, J.D. Salinger – who have prospered as authors partly because they could be touted as "personalities"' (162). And yet Boorstin skips quickly from these examples to a critique of 'best-sellerism,' the rage for best-selling, popular books. There is an inconsistency here. Hemingway, Mailer, and Salinger certainly were promoted as personalities (or perhaps, in the case of Salinger, as a non-personality), and yet each of them retained his appeal both to a fairly wide readership and, more emphatically, to a cultural elite. Boorstin seems to be lumping their situation together with the triumph of the best-seller, which is another situation entirely. Furthermore, when Boorstin critiques the best-seller, he does so from the vantage point of a strict demarcation between high and popular culture that does not acknowledge the sort of substantial overlap that is evident in figures such as Hemingway, Mailer, and Salinger. Instead, it is clear, to him, that a best-seller is necessarily an inferior book (167). Elsewhere in *The Image*, however, Boorstin complains that 'our idolized authors are esoteric ... Our most honored literati are only half-intelligible to nearly all the educated community' (55). Faced with these options – caving in to bestsellerism or scaling the ivory tower – it is difficult to see what a poor author is to do.

Boorstin's inheritors, Neil Postman and Neal Gabler, retain some of his critique of bestsellerism, but without the complaints of literary obscurantism in canonically high places. In *Life, the Movie*, Gabler basically replays Boorstin's criticism of best-seller culture, but he stops short of Boorstin's miscalculations about American personality authors; 'still,' he reminds his readers, 'Hemingway and Mailer had talent, and their personas as brawling artists ultimately depended upon it' (126). Realizing that only limited mileage for his thesis about the destructiveness of entertainment culture is to be had from the examples of celebrated writers who question precisely those boundaries between high and popular culture that Boorstin and Gabler himself depend upon, Gabler quickly changes the subject to celebrity authors (i.e., celebrities, such as Joan Collins, who happen to write books). Salman Rushdie's unfortunate celebrity he takes note of, but with the hasty assurance that he is 'a serious novelist' (128) and so presumably does not owe his celebrity to purely trashy causes. Clearly, these cracks and fault lines reveal that we need a theory of literary celebrity that does not need to divide the celebrity author into the high-culture personality artist and the crass-minded potboiling best-seller hack.

As ideological critics are aware, celebrity is, as Richard Dyer says, 'found across a range of media texts' (*Stars* 68), and ranking those texts or their authors hierarchically is very little to the purpose. Dyer is, for instance, aware of work in film studies that seeks to categorize star images according to particular archetypes – for example, the Good Joe, the Tough Guy, the Pin-Up – but he is wary of adopting that methodology because star images, in his view, are much more complex than types. So, too, with writers and the labels 'serious writer' and 'popular writer.' In dealing with this question in his study of American literary stars, Joe Moran draws on the concept of middlebrow culture as an alternative to such oppositional categories. He argues that literary celebrity in America was the 'product of a historically close relationship between certain kinds of authors and a "middlebrow" print culture, which was ultimately answerable to the marketplace but which also aimed to make literature accessible to the broader populace' (33–4). This intermediate positioning between the forces of cultural and economic capital is germane to my study of Canadian celebrity; all of the literary stars whom I examine in some detail in this volume are positioned in this way. Historically, the term middlebrow has been used to categorize and denounce literary celebrity from a vantage point of elite culture, and so I use the term with some trepidation. I see the placement of the writers I study here less as a static categorization than as a dynamic fluctuating between competing forces of cultural respect and economic success.

Stardom is porous not only in terms of artistic hierarchy or value, but also in terms of medium or discipline. As Christine Gledhill explains, building on Dyer's notion of the star text, the star 'crosses disciplinary boundaries.' Introducing a collection of celebrity from the perspective of film studies, Gledhill finds that it is important, by 1991, to say that stardom need not be limited to film (xiii). There is an awareness here that if she is going to take the implications of Dyer's definition of a star seriously, she needs to acknowledge that celebrity travels across disciplines and is doing so more and more (in fields like politics, for example). Still, Gledhill must acknowledge that, as of 1991, at least, 'cinema still provides the ultimate confirmation of stardom' (xiii). Three years later, in *Claims to Fame*, Joshua Gamson assumes this transferability of celebrity phenomena from film to other sites of cultural production; 'Understanding entertainment celebrity,' he argues, 'promises to help us comprehend celebrity as a general cultural phenomenon: its peculiar dynamics, its place in everyday lives, its broader implications' (5). This notion, that stardom is disciplinarily porous and migratory, is central to my analysis of literary celebrity, though it has become a contested idea of late in celebrity studies. As P. David Marshall argues, 'the disciplinary boundaries between the domains of popular culture and political culture have been eroded through the migration of communicative strategies and public relations from the entertainment industries to the organization of the spectacle of politics' (xiii). The argument need not be restricted to the entertainment and political spheres, however. It applies just as reasonably to the literary field of production and its links to entertainment culture. Unlike some cultural critics, however,

I will not be arguing that, in the past entertainment and literary culture were hermetically sealed and have only recently started to seep into each other; the boundaries have always been, to a degree, porous.

More recently, Graeme Turner has cautioned against transposing celebrity phenomena too readily from one medium to another. 'Tempting though these big connections are,' he writes in *Understanding Celebrity,* 'they tend to obscure the fact that what constitutes celebrity in one cultural domain may be quite different in another' (17). This caution is a valuable one, and in my own work on Canadian literary celebrity, I draw, from time to time, the necessary distinctions between a literary writer's renown and celebrity of the more celluloid variety. Still, I would offer a distinction between the sort of large-scale transposition that Turner criticizes (and Gamson, for one, seems comfortable with) and what I am describing as porosity. To say that celebrity systems are porous, that they allow, like a cell membrane, for osmosis as well as the maintenance of boundaries, is very different from saying that celebrity phenomena are unproblematically transferable from one cultural medium to another. It is precisely this condition of cultural porosity that I will seek to capture, in studying the particular shapes that celebrity assumes in the literary field.

Although there have been no major studies of literary celebrity in Canada, and very few in general, apart from studies of figures such as Hemingway, Dickens, and Twain, there is a large body of work on the whole issue of *who* gets star treatment in literary Canada – what one might call canonization studies. There is a substantial and absorbing field of criticism on why certain writers and not others have received attention throughout Canadian literary history (Robert Lecker's *Making It Real* and *Canadian Canons,* Frank Davey's *Canadian Literary Power,* and Carole Gerson's, *A Purer Taste,* to name a few examples). So, in a sense, there has been an implicit concern with literary celebrity in Canada. Almost all of these studies, however, perform the valuable task of pondering *who* gets chosen as one of the literary elect at particular historical moments in Canada and – more difficult to say – *why*. Or else they debate – another valuable objective – whether Canada can be said to have a canon at all, or whether it has multiple, competing canons; whether those canons are monolithic and hierarchical or regionally dispersed and laterally organized. My own work does not concern the who and why but, rather, the *how* of literary celebrity: how celebrity culture migrates and continues to migrate, in ever-changing forms, to the literary field; what forms it takes in literary production and marketing; and what the implications are for marketing and promoting Canadian writing.

Many suggestive aspects of this fascinating ongoing discussion of canonicity and Canadian literature prove valuable to my own interest in celebrity culture. When Lynette Hunter broaches the topic of the canonization of living authors, for example, she touches, briefly, on the object of my study: 'The speed with which these writings [of the 1960s and after] were authorized raises in an acute manner the related set of questions about what the canonization of a living author does to the work of that writer, and further how it affects the reader's response' (24). Hunter leaves it at that, but the tone is predominantly suspicious. It does not sound as though the canonization of a living author could have very many salutary effects. Such concerns participate in a familiar celebrity trope: the costs of sudden fame, which are always thought to increase the closer one approaches the present historical moment. It would be interesting to question, though, whether the canonization of living authors is that much of a post-1960s phenomenon, egged on by the recommendations of the Symons Report and the Mathews–Steele Report to give greater support to the publication of Canadian texts. That is why I historicize my own study of Ondaatje, Atwood and Shields by looking at the way in which earlier writers, specifically L.M. Montgomery, Pauline Johnson, Stephen Leacock, and Mazo de la Roche, experienced fame in their own lifetimes.

Frank Davey, on the other hand, in *Canadian Literary Power*, distinguishes between fame and literary activity in a way that usefully challenges my own sense of what, exactly, I am studying.

From the beginning of his book, Davey contrasts the showy, ephemeral Canadian literature publicity machine with the grassroots realities of Canadian literary activity: 'To a large extent, the prosperous, self-celebrating literary community of international prizes, Toronto media events, and photogenic faces that appear in journals like *Books in Canada* is a self-sustaining illusion, one that is increasingly disconnected from the disagreements Canadian writers have among each other, from the books that are chosen for academic reprint and study, and from the anthologies that are produced and reviewed in communities outside downtown Toronto' (i–ii). Davey's critique of the literary fame game is tempting, but the terms of the critique are questionable. Fame becomes associated with commercially decadent Central Canada, and real literary activity with the other regions of Canada, but to assume that the celebrity machine does not equally animate the other regions is to participate in a variety of pastoral idealism. International prizes, for example, are highly publicized outside of the area of the Golden Horseshoe, as the career of Carol Shields attests.

As Davey continues his analysis of Canadian literary power, he builds another distinction between fame and real literary activity that is implicitly placed over his contrast between Toronto and the Rest of Canada. He contrasts what he calls 'short-term interventions' 'on behalf of a text' 'that affect its immediate reception – radio and television appearances, newspaper and news magazine reviews that appear within the month of publication' – and the sort of intervention that signals a text's 'persistence in cultural memory' (106). Again, I sense that, for Davey, the media blitz is the work of Toronto and the authentic work of canonization happens mainly elsewhere. More important, Davey has reinscribed the popular culture–high culture dichotomy that causes difficulties for Postman, Gabler, and Boorstin's attempts to theorize celebrity. Fame is fleeting, canonization permanent. Although Davey is right, of course, that the book that is cried up this month in the book pages will not necessarily make it onto courses in Canadian literature in ten years, the categories are, like those of popular and high culture, much more

porous that they appear here. Both the recipient of warm publication notices and the household names participate, to some
degree, in literary celebrity, and the fates of both of those participants is open to change. The publicized first-time author
may indeed drop out of sight after that initial publication, but
so may the so-called canonized author of a few decades ago.
Witness Hugh MacLennan. How long celebrity is enjoyed may
be, for my purposes, slightly beside the point. Rather, the question is, what effects does it create when it is in operation?

    One positive effect of the renewed interest in canonization in
the last decade has been greater receptivity to economic analyses of Canadian literature, though it has been an uphill fight.
Critics of Canadian literature have been, in the past number of
decades, extremely reticent about the economic processes at
work in the formation of the literature and its canons, prefer-
ring to rely on universal abstractions such as good taste and
artistic excellence. In fact, I suspect that because Canadian literature courses came slowly to academic study and teaching in
this country, specialists in the field have always been loathe to
abandon the criteria of excellence. Decades ago, as they struggled to introduce CanLit courses, many of them faced the scepticism of their colleagues: was Canadian literature really good
enough? Having gained a foothold in university departments
because of the quality argument, specialists may have been wary
of letting it go. Mainly because of the canonization studies of
Davey, Lecker, Gerson, and the others, however, there is a
renewed interest, early in this new century, in the material production of Canadian literature: books, articles, special issues of
journals are appearing on the subject. Lynette Hunter, writing
her *Outsider Notes* as a teacher of Canadian literature in Britain,
is able to take the interconnectedness of the economic and the
scholarly for granted: 'What is undoubted is the intimate connection between canons and both educational establishments
and publishing economics' (23). In studying literary celebrity,
then, the role of 'publishing economics' is at the forefront,
rather than shunted off to the side as unworthy of scholarly
interest or value. In researching this book, for instance, I had to

update the files of information and writing about three Canadian writers I had taught or published on extensively before: Margaret Atwood, Michael Ondaatje, and Carol Shields. My files were full of academic articles from scholarly journals, references to books analysing their writing, and reviews. But in researching the topic of their celebrity I had to go back and retrieve those items that I had, first as a graduate student and then as a teacher of Canadian literature for twenty years, disregarded as not scholarly enough or simply irrelevant to what I saw as my primarily literary purpose: profiles of the writers in magazines and newspapers, detailed publishing figures, and advertisements for their books and for films based on their books. What was happening was a reorientation of what I was seeing as academically valuable, and the new orientation did not shut out the operations of publicity and publishing economies. For this reason, such journalistic sources will play a more visible role in this study than they usually do in academic publications.

In many ways, a similar remembering of the economic has taken place in celebrity studies. When he published *Stars*, Richard Dyer remarked that so many of the studies of individual celebrities that had preceded his book were anecdotal, relying upon untheorized notions of the stars' innate 'magic' (16); in sketching out the theories of production and consumption that offered a more systematic means of understanding stardom, he began by concentrating on economics (10), though he showed why a relentless focus on the celebrity as economic product would yield only a partial account of the formation of stars. Similarly, in *Understanding Celebrity*, Turner turns away from impressionistic concepts of celebrity, noting that 'celebrity is routinely treated as a domain of irrationality' (136). So often, he writes, economic factors such as 'publicity and promotions' are left out of accounts of celebrity, and that is unfortunate because 'when we conceptualise celebrity as something to be professionally managed, rather than discursively deconstructed, we think about it differently' (136). An exception to Turner's rule is Joshua Gamson's *Claims to Fame*, which departs from many of the previous studies of celebrity by focusing, in some detail, on the roles of agents, publicists, journalists, and institutional sponsors. His analysis is all the more striking for having arrived, like the analysis of economics in Canadian literature, relatively late on the scene.

As I have remarked, many writers on celebrity and its literary manifestations have tended to differentiate between high and popular culture, and many Canadian literature scholars have bypassed a full recognition of the economic in coming to terms with their field. A theorist whose work managed to address literary production and canonization without doing either one of these things was the French sociologist Pierre Bourdieu. As such, his work represents the closest to a comprehensive theoretical foundation for my own study of Canadian literary celebrity. In *The Field of Cultural Production*, the book that is germane to my purposes, Bourdieu deals with the dilemma with which I opened this discussion: is literary celebrity power really powerful enough to classify as stardom? Rather than placing fields of cultural endeavour on a bar graph and measuring their power in any one-dimensional way, Bourdieu argues that the literary or artistic field is contained by what he calls 'the field of power' in a society, which means, generally speaking, the relations of economic and political power. Still, the literary field, according to Bourdieu, possesses 'a relative autonomy with respect to it [the field of power], especially as regards its economic and political principles of hierarchization' (37–8). So the literary field is, obviously, affected by the workings of economy and profit, but it may also establish some autonomous procedures of its own. For example, within what Bourdieu calls 'the field of restricted production,' or what we might call high art, art that is produced for fewer people, a different kind of capital is stocked: cultural capital, which basically means literary prestige or respectability. Avant-garde artists, to choose Bourdieu's most extreme example, may pride themselves on how few consumers of their art they have, since their distance from mass consumption marks a certain artistic superiority – assurance that they are on the 'cutting edge.' So wondering whether literary celebrity is powerful enough is beside the point, since the power of literary celebrity operates within the field of literary production, maintains some ties to economic imperatives issuing from the field of power, but also proceeds by some of its own tendencies or game rules.

Bourdieu's characterization of a 'field of restricted production,' which stands in distinction to a 'field of large-scale production' (what we might call popular art, or art produced for many consumers), might make it seem that he, too, is caught up in the same dichotomizing as Boorstin, Postman, or Gabler. But this dichotomy operates differently. Bourdieu is careful to point out that the boundaries between the two fields are porous: some exclusive authors may not be esteemed and 'some box-office successes may be recognized, at least in some sectors of the field, as genuine art' (39). Furthermore, he does not seal off symbolic capital, which he says producers in the fields of restricted production seek, from other forms of capital, such as economic profits, which are more habitually associated with the field of large-scale production. He points out that 'symbolic capital is to be understood as economic or political capital that is disavowed, misrecognized and thereby recognized, hence legitimate, a "credit" which, under certain conditions, and always in the long run, guarantees "economic" profits' (75). This point speaks directly to my uneasiness with Davey's distinction between inauthentic Toronto-centred commercial publicity and authentic grassroots literary activity, since the symbolic capital that is presumably built up in the process of the regional, decentralized canonization that he perceives at work across the country does not shut out the workings of other kinds of capital. Even avant-garde artists, Bourdieu argues, rely in some senses upon other, economic forms of capital, ironic though that may seem. After all, only those in a society who are economically stable, or drawn from economically stable classes, usually have the freedom to take up 'risky positions' in the artistic world, positions that 'secure no short-term profit' (67). So symbolic capital is capital in denial; it is the economic capital that dare not speak its name.

This double-mindedness is very much like the resistance to the economic that I have described in Canadian academic literary circles. In describing how it operates in cultural businesses, Bourdieu comes closest to an explicit discussion of celebrity. As a sociologist, however, he readily looked for his starting point to an earlier sociologist: Max Weber. Implicitly drawing on Weber's notion of charisma, a concept that is, as both Richard Dyer and P. David Marshall have recognized, an important early component of celebrity, Bourdieu notes that 'the "charismatic" ideology ... directs attention to the *apparent producer*, the painter, writer or composer, in short the "author," suppressing the question of what authorizes the author, what creates the authority with which authors authorize' (76). Here Bourdieu is drawing on the influential authorship theories of Michel Foucault in 'What Is an Author?' or the socialized vision of authorship offered by Raymond Williams in *Marxism and Literature*. Bourdieu's description of the charismatic ideology recalls what I observed earlier about the spectacle of the celebrity author tending to reinforce the naively autobiographical connection between author and text that most authors today would prefer to avoid. Far from being merely false consciousness, however, charisma or celebrity is itself deeply rooted in economic capital and its motives. The film star, after all, writes John Ellis, was a 'marketing strategy' that arrived 'at the point at which the initial expansion of cinema had taken place' (92), and the star helped viewers to distinguish films from each other and give them consumable trademarks.

Are authors of literary works, then, no more than consumable trademarks once they enter the culture of celebrity? According to Foucault and Bourdieu, perhaps they have never not been consumable trademarks to a certain extent, authorship being, as Foucault – and Derrida – have argued, a shorthand (or trademark) for a conglomeration of texts. But all of the authors I will study as celebrities have given voice to sceptical treatments of celebrity culture while participating to varying degrees in that culture. It is as though they, like Bourdieu's notion of cultural capital, are participating in that which they deny. As Pauline Johnson, literary star performer par excellence, wrote to a concerned friend at the end of the nineteenth century, 'More than all things I hate and despise brain debasement, literary "pot-boiling" and yet I have done, will do these things, though I sneer at my own littleness in so doing. Believe me, it is not a degraded choice' (qtd. Keller, *Pauline: A Biography* 72). Johnson's conflictedness resurfaces in our literary history whenever a writer becomes a celebrity and discovers that he or she must constantly negotiate the seemingly exclusive worlds of popularity and literary prestige. Writers such as Margaret Atwood, Michael Ondaatje, and Carol Shields cannot help but participate, if ambivalently, in what Ondaatje once dubbed 'the twentieth-century game of fame.'

2 Earlier Literary Stardom in Canada

Each new generation of literary stars has struggled with the perception that their stardom is somehow inauthentic or unearned, that it is a product of publicity machines, the decline of public taste, or a host of other imagined cultural ills. And yet those earlier generations of writers who supposedly provide the standard of earned, authentic literary value have themselves had to struggle with the competing claims of popularity and literary prestige, economic and symbolic capital. So, to counter the sort of notion that a follower of the Postman–Gabler school of cultural criticism would support, that current literary celebrity somehow marks a decline from a golden age of genuine literary value, I offer and consider the following selected examples of earlier Canadian literary celebrity: Pauline Johnson, Stephen Leacock, Mazo de la Roche, and Lucy Maud Montgomery. Each one of them struggled mightily with the attractions of economic and symbolic forms of literary capital, and they formulated a variety of responses, sometimes contradictory ones, to that struggle.

In tracing their struggles, decisions, and accommodations, I depart from the pervasive myth that celebrated Canadian intellectual figures, for whatever reason, have tended to be unaffected or unspoiled by fame. Clarence Karr, in his foundational study of popular Canadian authorship in the early twentieth century, embraces this myth, positing as he does so, the image of the Canadian as the culturally unaffected innocent. Writing of Nellie McClung, L.M. Montgomery, Ralph Connor, and Arthur Stringer, Karr observes that in 'spite of all the fame and fortune experienced by these four authors ... they remained essentially unchanged. Perhaps because they were Canadian, they exhibited little pretension; there was no "putting on airs," no inflated egos. Although their lifestyles improved, there would be no exotic, international vacations ... They all remained conventional, middle-class Canadians' (56–7). In short, they didn't *really* become celebrities, not in that global sense of stardom that we have inherited from Hollywood culture, because it is just not in the nature of Canadian cultural icons, those wide-eyed innocents, to become worldly, to be changed by fame. Though that may be truer of Karr's examples, particularly Stringer and Connor, it is less true of other earlier Canadian literary celebrities, such as Pauline Johnson, whose fame reified her as a commodifiable 'Mohawk Princess' for non-Native consumption, or Stephen Leacock, whose fame was caught up in his obsessive drive for conspicuously displayed commodities (money, houses) that would provide him with reassuring evidence of his intrinsic worth. Even Lucy Maud Montgomery, though she ostensibly played the unchanging role of a dutiful minister's wife in Ontario during the same years that an international readership eagerly awaited her next book, was riven by the doubleness of her identity as L.M. Montgomery and Mrs Ewan Macdonald.

The opposite position – that fame was a determining factor in the evolution of Canadian literature as an entity – has recently been formulated in Nick Mount's book *When Canadian Literature Moved to New York*. Mount argues that, for the writers of the 1890s and 1900s, fame was the siren's call that led a whole generation of Canadian writers to pursue their trade south of the border. These writers, according to Mount, read about the attentions showered on America literary celebrities such as Richard Harding Davis or journalists Joseph Pulitzer and William Randolph Hearst, and they wished for a part of this celebrity action: 'Bread could be had in Canada; fame was the province of elsewhere. And Canadian writers chose elsewhere'

(31). Many, of course, did not, and one criticism of Mount's argument is that he tends to overstate the magnitude of this considerable literary exodus. Stephen Leacock, for instance, made a determined choice to stay in Canada, and yet his fame in the United States was, and remains, a force to be reckoned with. Still, Mount's study is a welcome corrective to the assumption that Canadian writers of this period shunned fame or were somehow above coveting it. Writers of the time had to feel the attractions of a much larger English-language market, well-established urban literary communities, and attractive copyright laws next door (27). Fame, then, is a much more powerful force in the history of Canadian literature than has been suspected, and its possessors have not been blasé about or unaffected by its workings in their careers and lives.

My examples of early literary celebrities, like Karr's, are all drawn from the period between the 1890s and the early decades of the twentieth century. (The most long-lived was de la Roche, whose life and writing career stretched to 1960, well after the period in which she obtained and was in main possession of her fame.) Even though literary renown was by no means unknown in Canadian circles before 1890, there are important reasons why both Karr and I are drawn to this period for our studies. As Karr points out, the 1890s marked 'the beginnings of a cultural golden age for Canadians in which a mass market opened' for a number of writers and 'the concept of "best-seller" firmly entrenched itself in the consciousness of publishers, booksellers, and readers' (26). In his valuable historical study, Karr carefully traces why all of this came to pass in the 1890s: the increasing industrialization of book publishing (26–7), the growth of advertising in the book trade (28), and the strengthening of copyright laws that would protect Canadian authors from the main threat to their economic health, cheap American pirated editions (30). To this institutional analysis, I would also add the growth, during exactly the same period, of an industrialized entertainment industry that culminated, in North American culture, in the heyday of Hollywood in the 1920s. Discourses of fame were being transformed, and the notion, in particular, of the overnight success, along with the mass consumption of cultural materials necessarily had an effect upon the ways in which fame was constructed in other cultural fields like literature, music, and sport.

Karr refers to this period as the golden age of popular Canadian fiction, one that he sees as interrupted by the advent of literary modernism, with its strict demarcations between high or elite culture and popular culture. In fact, he argues that although 'Van Wyck Brooks coined the terms "highbrow" and "lowbrow" in 1915 to distinguish between this new, popular, bestseller type of culture and the older, more elite culture ... many North Americans had not yet engaged in such departmentalization' (33). Karr cites the activities of literary societies in the late nineteenth and early twentieth centuries throughout North America, societies that, Karr argues, were able to take in all points on the spectrum that ran from popular fiction to Shakespeare. In numerous critical readings of authors such as Montgomery and de la Roche, Canadian literary scholars agree with this basic scenario, crediting the rise of modernist aesthetics with the growing distaste for popular fiction (Gerson, 'The Most Canadian'). Although there is a great deal of truth in this assertion, and much that explains the decline in the literary fortunes of all four of the authors I discuss here, the golden age and decline model must be more closely interrogated and refined if it is to prove useful in analysing the role of literary celebrity during these years. To say that modernism brought with it a split between high and popular culture (or, in Bourdieu's terms, between proponents of the 'field of restricted production' and the 'field of large-scale production') is to underestimate the rivalry between the two that existed before the advent of literary modernism. In the early 1890s, for instance, Pauline Johnson was warned by a friend that her newfound success as a performing recitalist had its cultural dangers, and that she was denigrating herself and her art by deigning to perform it dramatically. Of course, embedded in this caution was the fear of contamination by the disreputability of the stage, even though elocution was thought to be a genteel, acceptable mode of performance for middle-class women. Johnson reacted by earning enough money from her performances to have her first book of poems published, thus using the fruits of her labour in the field of large-scale production to ensure herself a coveted space in the field of restricted production. Throughout my readings of these earlier literary stars, therefore, I will resist the temptation to see the high culture–popular culture divide as purely a product of modernism. Modernism no doubt empha-sized and widened it, but it did not herald its advent and bring to an end a golden age of easy exchange between high and pop-ular culture. All four of the authors I study here felt the anxiety of the clash of forms of cultural capital most painfully well before the heyday of literary modernism in Canada reduced scholarly interest in their works. Modernism simply exacerbated their anxiety.

Another model of golden age and decline that canonization studies in Canada have challenged is that of the economic disin-terestedness of earlier literary classics. In this model, it is assumed that the earlier works in national canons have some-how come down to us because of an inherent virtue or quality that sets them apart from more recent literary products that cir-culate in the literary market. The most striking example of the challenge to this idea is Robert Lecker's examination of McClel-land and Stewart's New Canadian Library editions, the reissue series that brought affordable, accessible Canadian texts into the classroom and enabled the institutionalized teaching of Canadian literature in the 1960s. Working against a powerful tradition that argues that the books in this series embodied some form of collective consciousness or inherited tradition, Lecker argues, instead, that the series editors, Jack McClelland and Malcolm Ross, often made their choices based on what was least expensive to buy or what was already in the public domain: 'Ross and McClelland had to confront the reality faced by all anthologists: the fact that what gets reprinted and collected is a direct function of cost and availability. Canons are often the product of market forces, and they always transmit an ideology that is market-centered. Not all readers know this; consequently they may be led to assume that the "classics" before them are somehow uncontaminated by the market when, in reality, it is precisely this contamination that determines a large part of their value' (23). The point is similar to the one Bourdieu makes about the field of extremely specialized literary production, such as symbolist poetry: deriving value from its apparent economic disinterestedness, it is nevertheless enabled by considerable economic support and underpinning. Similarly, in the readings of the literary celebrities of the early twentieth century that I offer here, economic pressures loom large, the better to correct the criticism that, somehow, present-day book publishing is driven by the market whereas earlier works in our national canons, issuing from an economically innocent age, have somehow been freer of this sort of contamination.

My choice of these four examples of literary celebrity from Canada's past is based, then, on two broad initiatives: to show how celebrity was not necessarily passed off or ignored by the stereotypically unpretentious, unaffected Canadian, and to dramatize how forcefully Canadian literary celebrities were divided and driven by the competing imperatives of cultural prestige and popular success. Besides, all four literary figures, to my mind, best exemplify the definition of stardom growing out of film and television studies that I have found most suggestive for my (literary) purposes: the idea of the star as a performer whose image circulates beyond the original area of specialization. Although the literary performances of these four writers may be safely assumed to rest in the past, their star image, as Richard Dyer would say, has circulated widely among cultural fields of various sorts and continues to do so: festivals named in their honour, literary homes turned into thriving tourist sites, television and film adaptations, and many other representations in popular and educational culture. Though other writers of the time achieved similar successes in terms of books sold, few of them, in my view, have travelled so far in cultural terms as have these four stars.

There was no doubt about the applicability of the term 'star' to the career of Pauline Johnson. In fact, she used the term to refer to herself, signing letters to her promoter, Frank Yeigh, 'Your Star' (Keller, *Pauline: A Biography* 65). As a performer (rather than simply a reciter) of her poems and stories, she was given star billing in her numerous appearances throughout North America and England, as shown in publicity posters for her second tour in England, which featured, in large letters, her Mohawk name 'Tekahionwake' ('Miss E. Pauline Johnson' in parentheses below), over a large, striking photograph of the poet in profile. The name of Johnson's long-time partner on the stage, 'Mr. Walter McRaye, Humorist,' appeared at the bottom of the page, at a distinct remove from the star attraction. In a humorous photographic representation of this pecking order, another publicity shot of the two performers shows a rather bemused looking McRaye posed lying at Johnson's feet. As Sheila Johnston comments, 'The curious pose, of Walter reclining at the feet of the star, Pauline, defines their partnership' (177). Other publicity shots call upon the recognizable iconography of stage stardom of the day; one, a collage of photographs that appeared in the *Globe* in the early days of her celebrity, in 1894, shows a ring of publicity shots of Johnson, mostly in stylish evening or day dress (only one featuring her constructed version of Mohawk dress), surrounding a central oval studio portrait of Johnson in an elegant wrap, wearing a tiara. Although a great deal of recent critical interest has focused on Johnson's negotiation and performance of her two ethnic identities, there seems little doubt that when she was performing the identity of stage star, it was her non-Native heritage that came to the fore and was served up for presentation to her non-Native audiences. Stardom, predictably, disrupted the balanced negotiation of Johnson's ethnic identities.

Johnson's career on the stage so overwhelmed her work as a publishing poet that many of the celebrity motifs that mark her literary career seem directly imported from the stage and the screen. Of these, the narrative of sudden success – 'a star is born' – is the most pervasive. Almost all of the critics and biographers who survey Johnson's career in any detail draw attention to the recital she gave at the Young Men's Liberal Club of

Toronto on 16 January 1892, at which she recited her poetry so movingly that her performance was met with thunderous applause. Sheila Johnston, in her account of this evening, makes the theatrical metaphor explicit: 'Her recitation so startled and moved the audience that, in the finest tradition of theatrical lore, a star was born. Pauline entered the collective Canadian conscience that evening, and she never left it' (98). Betty Keller uses the narration of that night to open her 1999 popular biography of Johnson; from that opening chapter, 'The Star of the Show,' Keller moves back in time to trace Johnson's life and career, starting with her family history in Brantford, Ontario. All paths, it seems, lead to the stereotypical life-changing, star-making performance. Even Keller, however, like other more recent critics of Johnson, has revealed this narrative for what it is: a well-worn celebrity cliché that obscures the actual facts of Johnson's earlier literary activities. In the longer biography of Johnson that she wrote in 1981, Keller pointed out that Johnson's promoter Frank Yeigh, did much to advance 'the story that Pauline had been an "instant recitalist," suddenly transformed from "the bashful and frightened Indian princess-maiden" to an assured platform performer' (*Pauline: A Biography* 59). As Keller sardonically notes, 'Yeigh's instant recitalist story must have amused the people of Brantford and Hamilton who had seen Pauline perform from time to time over the preceding seven years' (ibid.). More recently, in their substantial study of Johnson, *Paddling Her Own Canoe*, Veronica Strong-Boag and Carole Gerson observe that, in addition to previous recitals that Johnson had given, she was 'quite familiar not only in the Toronto press, but also to readers of the *Canadian Magazine*, and *Dominion Illustrated* and Brantford newspapers' (103). So, as is usually the case, the birth of the star was a more protracted labour than the well-worn celebrity cliché suggests.

Strong-Boag and Gerson read Yeigh's discovery narrative in a postcolonial mode, noting that it 'fits into the colonial paradigm, in which he [Yeigh] performs the role of patriarchal European explorer, while she serves as the feminized indigenous "virgin land" awaiting his intervention and identification of her value' (103). This is undoubtedly true. Yeigh's narrative also partakes, however, of an increasingly popular discourse of celebrity discovery that was about to gain force in North America with the rise of the motion picture industry, a discourse that is also permeated by colonizing impulses (most obviously when one considers genres such as the western). What is important for my purposes, however, is the way in which this particular form of celebrity discourse obscures apprenticeship. As Richard Dyer has observed of fan magazines, their representations of stars' lives as consisting mainly of leisure activities obscures 'the fact that making films is work' (*Stars* 39). So too with literary celebrities from Johnson to Atwood, the sudden-fame motif obscures the fact of an often long, hard period of apprenticeship work.

The factor of star visibility, the idea that celebrities must necessarily consign to the public realm aspects of themselves that they might prefer to remain private, was as evident in the celebrity of Pauline Johnson as it is in contemporary stardom. As Strong-Boag and Gerson argue, Johnson's star visibility may have taken certain private options or decisions out of her hands altogether. Citing the possibility for Metis women of Johnson's time and before to 'pass' as a non-Native settler in a marriage to a non-Native man, they note that this was not possible for Johnson: 'Unlike many other Mixed-race women ... she became far too famous to set aside readily the racial heritage that the age frequently considered problematic and to reappear as a respectable settler matron' (68). Having made the decision to perform her mixed heritage publicly, Johnson was denied the option of performing either racial identity privately to the apparent exclusion of the other.

This sort of heightened public scrutiny also limited Johnson's ability to present herself as having evolved into a professional artist. Because much of her 'instant' fame depended precisely upon a presentation of Johnson as a culturally innocent child of nature to a non-Native audience, when Johnson did hone her professional stage skills, audiences reacted with disappointment. Betty Keller reveals that by 1902, audiences found

Johnson more professional, less innocent-seeming, and she correctly ascribes their negative response to the workings of celebrity culture: 'It is the fate of those rising to fame from obscure beginnings to be constantly examined by their public for signs of change. They are expected to remain unaltered even thought the most pedestrian personality within the common mass is allowed to lose innocence and become hardened and moulded by the stresses of life. But a celebrity is victim of the I-knew-her-when game, and it always turns out that she was a nicer individual when they knew her' (*Pauline: A Biography* 191). In turn, this celebrity phenomenon is cross-constructed by variables of race and gender; in addition to her audience's expectations that Johnson remain some version of the naive child of nature, they also expected a late-Victorian woman, as a supposed inhabitant of the private sphere, to remain untouched by exposure to public life.

If increased public scrutiny brought with it a diminished repertoire of life performances in some respects, it also allowed for special rules and dispensations that expanded the limits of what was possible for Pauline Johnson. Keller points to Johnson's brief engagement with Charles Drayton, a man eleven years her junior, as an example of a type of relationship that late-Victorian Canadian society would have disapproved of in the case of a non-celebrity, but the 'public made a special allowance ... for one category of female: the celebrity who married a younger man' (*Pauline: A Biography* 134). Keller cites the examples of actress Lillie Langtry and socialite Jenny Churchill, among others. So here we have the paradoxical relation of celebrity to personal agency or power: like the stereotypical film star who does not have the privacy or freedom to walk down a street unmolested but whose brushes with the law are likely to result in lighter punishment, Johnson found that celebrity was both a restriction and a ticket of passage.

After Johnson's death, her star visibility continued to shape the way in which her career has been understood. As a number of critics have recently pointed out, discussions of Johnson to date have emphasized her biography, her personal star narra-

tive, at the expense of her writing (Stevenson). Reviewing
Strong-Boag and Gerson's *Paddling Her Own Canoe*, Janice Fiamengo opens by observing that 'scholars have usually been
more interested in Johnson's life than in her writing or the content of her stage performances' (174), a trend that she sees the
authors as reversing. George W. Lyon argues that such a biographical obsession seems inevitable with Johnson, because she
tended to 'mine her own past for content and for image' and
'asserted that her genetic history gave her the privilege of
addressing certain subjects' (136). There is a point here, even if
it does tend towards the reductive; Johnson's star image tended
to represent Johnson herself as a subject of her discourse and of
her theatrical presentation, the embodiment of that self on
stage. Again, as with the exercise of personal power within
celebrity, that image freed Johnson to signify on her identity in
her works and on stage, but it also acted as a restrictive force,
tempting audiences and later generations of critics to see her
biography as both the starting point and the horizon of her art.

The negative manifestations of fame in turn-of-the-century
Canada went beyond the merely restrictive. In the stereotypical
fashion of current celebrity culture, with its narratives of star
suicides and drug addictions, fame was often invoked as a
destroyer. Nowhere in Canadian literary history of the period is
this more emphatically the case than in representations of
Pauline Johnson. As Peter Unwin maintains, the 'standard critical line on Pauline Johnson is that of a young talent destroyed
by a career of travel and stage recitations' (19). Certainly she
often presented herself as being at the mercy of her celebrity; in
a letter that she wrote describing how she had to go on stage
instead of travelling to her brother's funeral, she bitterly
described herself as 'the mere doll of the people and slave to
money' (qtd. Johnston 126). Loss of control is at the basis of
many of these representations of fame as a destroyer. Film theorist James Monaco has suggested that 'control is obviously a
major determinant in the celebrity formula' (12), and, in that
spirit, he has categorized stardom in terms of the degree of control that a celebrity has over his or her stardom. 'Quasars,' in his

typology, are stars who 'almost never have any real control over the image they project' (11). In many stories about Johnson, this lack of control over image resurfaces as a major motif. Sheila Johnston, for instance, recounts the remembrance, of one of Johnson's friends, Jean Stevinson, from near the end of · Johnson's life: '"Fame is nothing, Tommy," she told me one day. "Remember, it's not worth that!" snapping her fingers in front of me. But she could not stem fame, which was to roll and billow around her' (216).

An influential critical interpretation of Pauline Johnston is built upon a similar perception of her relationship to fame: the idea that, like a quasar, she ultimately lost control over her self-representations and, instead, slavishly fed her public whatever image they desired. This argument lies at the heart of Daniel Francis's analysis of Johnson as one of the forms of 'imaginary Indian' he calls the 'celebrity Indian.' This figure is, like the quasar, a star who has lost control over his or her signification. As Francis explains, a celebrity Indian 'gains a wide audience among non-Natives, who then project onto it the voice of the "typical Indian" in the non-Native imagination' (109). Besides Pauline Johnson, Grey Owl and Long Lance are Francis's paradigmatic Canadian examples of the celebrity Indian. Like many recent critics of Johnson, Francis sees her as caught between two desires: her avowed project of representing 'the glories of my own people' (qtd. Francis 116) and her need to satisfy a non-Native audience's preconceptions about Native people. As a result of this dilemma, Francis argues, Johnson was 'ambivalent about her Indian "image"' (116), and this ambivalence, in effect, destroyed her career: 'This need to satisfy the demands of a White audience stultified Pauline Johnson's development as a writer and limited her effectiveness as a spokesperson for Native people' (120). Critics might disagree about the extent to which Johnson was muzzled by her fame, but the fact remains that, far from having little effect upon the popular writers of the time in Canada as Karr suggests, fame was a key variable in how those writers interacted with their audiences.

Amid all the negative connotations and reflections that fill theoretical and critical discussions of celebrity, it sometimes needs to be recalled that celebrity can also bring pleasure, that it is as frequently enjoyed as it is decried as the destroyer of privacy, happiness, and personal freedom. As Strong-Boag and Gerson note, touring exhausted and sometimes frustrated Johnson, but 'she frequently appears to have enjoyed the new experiences and new people, not to mention the fame, which stage life brought' (79). Again, fame could act as a liberating as well as a restrictive force; as the authors aptly observe, fame allowed Johnson to participate 'in the beginning of a period of independent travel for women' (79), in a way that a woman of her class could not otherwise have done. There were other, less noble, pleasures afforded by fame; as Betty Keller notes, Johnson 'revelled in being lionized by the wealthy' in her tours across Canada, and she would manage to stay in the finest hotels no matter how full her concert halls were (*Pauline: A Biography* 106–7). In fact, Keller is rather sceptical about Johnson's famous outcry against the 'literary "pot-boiling"' and 'brain debasement' that her popularity forced upon her; she argues that Johnson continued to perform not just because she wanted to finance her first book of poetry but because she 'had discovered that she needed the limelight. She loved the applause, the recognition in the streets, the bouquets of flowers from admirers, the special status of the star' (ibid. 73–4).

It was that very status, however enjoyable it was for Johnson, that ensured her decline in the country's literary canons. Pauline Johnson is, indeed, a perfect example of Bourdieu's reflections on the way in which an artist's accumulation of economic capital tends to deplete any symbolic or cultural capital that he or she has managed to build up over a career. Carole Gerson's article 'The Most Canadian of All Canadian Poets" charts this inverse evolution of popularity and prestige in some detail. Calling to mind Earle Birney's mid-century dismissal of Johnson ('I don't read her'), Gerson argues that Birney, 'having read Pauline Johnson's identity as the commodified Indian princess of popular culture ... rejected the notion that her poetry could deserve his attention' (93). One of the reasons why modernists such as Birney dismissed Johnson, according to Gerson, was their 'conflicted attitude toward material success' (95), the same conflict that Bourdieu discerns in the fields of cultural production when producers of large-scale cultural productions (popular art) are '*symbolically* excluded and discredited' because they are making profits rather than stocking up on symbolic capital (39, emphasis Bourdieu's). Gerson makes this conflict between popularity and prestige clear: 'To the mind of the academic modernist, poetry presented in costumed performances aimed at audiences of the semi-washed could not possibly inhabit the same realm as poetry published in small university-based magazines' – one of the classic venues of Bourdieu's field of restricted production ('The Most Canadian' 96). Even in Johnson's day, according to Mary Elizabeth Leighton, reviewers of her written poetry dismissed the dramatic first-person performance poems that 'guaranteed box-office returns for her performances' in favour of 'her plotless landscape descriptions' in her lyrical nature poems (153). Strong-Boag and Gerson also report that from 1892 onward, 'Johnson's literary work was almost always received and assessed in relation to her performance,' whether the intent was to praise the written works by associating them with the material success of her performances, or to denigrate the texts by contamination with large-scale (and therefore non-serious) production (117). So even well before the heyday of modernism, Johnson's celebrity occasioned a conflicted response towards material success and a hasty juggling of the values of symbolic and economic capital.

The decline that Johnson's work experienced, therefore, was, as Strong-Boag and Gerson phrase it, 'a dramatic downward slide' 'at the level of elite culture' (122). As Gerson points out elsewhere, however, that narrative of decline must be read against a narrative of persistence at the level of popular culture, a 'presence that kept her books in print and preserved her name in schools and schoolbooks, a chocolate company, and almost in a major Vancouver theatre' ('The Most Canadian' 91). Recent scholars, such as Melanie Stevenson are pursuing the way in which Johnson persisted in these popular and pedagogical forms – in educational materials, for instance. The power of Johnson's star image to transfer itself to other media has been considerable, even at the time that most critics have spoken of her as forgotten or neglected. 'Johnson's name,' Strong-Boag and Gerson add, has 'been attached to a machine-gun' as well as a 'luxury yacht' (12), and, in 1961, she became the first Canadian author to have her image commemorated on a Canadian postage stamp (Gerson, 'The Most Canadian' 90). Generalized descriptions of Johnson's decline, therefore, need to be specified as issuing from the realm of high culture; at the level of popular culture, Pauline Johnson the celebrity was never absent.

The fame of Stephen Leacock has fared less well than that of Johnson or Lucy Maud Montgomery over the years, on both the popular and the elite levels. There is no major critical revival or reinvestigation of his work, as there has been of Johnson's and Montgomery's in recent years, and the heritage site at Leacock's home at Old Brewery Bay in Orillia, Ontario, has had a more troubled history and less fanfare than the celebrated Anne of Green Gables house in Cavendish, Prince Edward Island. Still, in the years following Leacock's success with *Literary Lapses* in 1910, there is no doubt that he was constructed as a star and that, in turn, he constructed himself as a star in various, sometimes conflicting, ways. As David Staines writes, 'In his own time, Leacock was the most famous Canadian author both at home and abroad. Sales of his books of humour, as well as his textbooks, were phenomenal' (1). By 1922, with the publication of the book that would win him the Governor General's Award, *My Discovery of England,* Leacock was 'a full-fledged international celebrity' (Doyle 52), a successful platform speaker, a writer whose works were already translated into several languages, and a commercial success. Attempts to market his Orillia home as a tourist site have featured such claims about Leacock's fame. The Parks Canada Web page for the Stephen Leacock Museum / Old Brewery Bay National Historic Site of Canada uses the term 'famous' twice in a short, one-hundred word paragraph (Parks Canada), and a late 1960s brochure for the house advertizes it as the site 'where Canada's most famous humorist lived and worked' ('Appendix to a Preliminary Study'). So, seemingly unequivocal claims of celebrity were made for Leacock both during and after his life, but a closer look at exactly what this fame consisted of discloses a number of tensions and ironies at work.

These are certainly evident in Leacock's star image, which was so powerful a force that it has challenged many a biographer to demystify it. It was an image uncannily similar to that of the great American humorist to whom Leacock was and is often compared: Mark Twain. Albert and Theresa Moritz describe the later Leacock persona in terms that would easily fit the elderly cracker-barrel philosopher persona of Samuel Clemens: 'a gray-haired, stoop-shouldered, wrinkled but smiling country sage' (10). As James Doyle suggests, Leacock had a whole repertoire of star personas that he could synthesize or assume as the occasion demanded: 'Leacock enjoyed his status as Canada's best-known literary figure. Always an inveterate actor, he presented a public image that was partly a satirical portrait of the typical academic as described in his "Apology of a Professor," partly a picture of the eccentric and indefatigable author, and partly a sketch of the country farmer of Orillia' (52). This light-and-sound show of identities may be frustrating for biographers, but it has turned out to be a boon for literary marketers. As Heather Kirk reports in an article on the fortunes of the Leacock House in Orillia, the 'Leacock persona' has provided a handy hook for organizers of the annual Leacock Heritage Festival. The shambling, aw-shucks-ma'am figure of the humorist allows for ready imitation and exploitation. In short, Leacock becomes a logo, a 'genteel Mickey Mouse in straw hat and cufflinks,' as Kirk satirically observes. And although the drawing power of this literary logo may not equal that of Montgomery and Prince Edward Island, it nevertheless brings well over a million tourist dollars to Orillia every summer.

As the constant comparisons of Leacock to Twain suggest, the variable of nationality is another pressure point in Leacock's celebrity. In fact, when plans were made to upgrade and promote the Old Brewery Bay house as a tourist site, calculations of Leacock's American appeal played a major role. As the Janus Museum Consultants, hired in the late sixties to do a feasibility study noted in their report, in 'the United States, Leacock is ranked with Mark Twain and is perhaps more recognized as a writer of importance in literary and academic circles there than in Canada' (3). Similarly, McGill University, for whom Leacock taught for many years before he was forced to retire, was, in essence, embarrassed into creating lasting memorials to Leacock on campus because of the numbers of American tourists who came to McGill inquiring where its memorial to Leacock was (Legate 251). The university, ashamed that there was, in the late fifties and early sixties, nothing to direct their American guests to, responded three-fold with the construction of the Leacock building for the social sciences, a special Leacock room in the MacLennan Library, and a memorial spot in the Faculty Club, where Leacock's apparently much-used chair sits below an oil portrait of the famous professor. To a considerable extent, then, American tourism has driven the Canadian memorialization of Stephen Leacock.

As Beverly Rasporich has pointed out, there has been an academic as well as a touristic battle of the nations over Leacock and his legacy. She traces the way in which critics of American humour have tended to claim Leacock as 'an originator of the twentieth-century comic figure of the "little man"' (77), who finds his way into numerous American cultural texts from those of Charlie Chaplin to those of Woody Allen, a powerless, bumbling everyman who is at the mercy of unsympathetic forces, whether bureaucratic or domestic. Because American critics see Leacock as the forefather of this 'American mainstream of little-man humour,' they have tended to 'consider Leacock one of their own' (78). There is, however, a tradition of counter-assertive Canadian criticism of Leacock, to which Rasporich herself contributes, that argues for the specifically Canadian mindset of Leacock's humour and his comic persona. Again, it seems as though this line of criticism, like the building of touristic shrines to 'Canada's most famed humorist' (Rasporich 77) has, ironically, been   driven by the power of American cultural claims upon Leacock.

Beyond the workings of elite cultural production in America, there was, in Leacock's case, a more popular reason for his popularity south of the border. President Theodore Roosevelt apparently did a great deal to bring Leacock before the American public simply by quoting him. The quotation in question is from 'Gertrude the Governess,' in which Lord Ronald 'flung himself upon his horse and rode madly off in all directions.' This has become one of the most oft-quoted passages from Leacock, I suspect largely because of its presidential seal of approval. David Legate, writing of this phenomenon, compares it to John F. Kennedy's starting of a vogue for Ian Fleming's spy stories by off-handedly mentioning, on one occasion, that James Bond was one of the president's favourite fictional characters (55). The scenario is a familiar one in American culture; one might add President Ronald Reagan's transformation of Tom Clancy from a successful writer to a literary star, simply by the act of holding up a copy of Clancy's *Red October* before the cameras (Cherney and Bailey Nurse A3). Sometimes, however, the process of presidential star-conferring misfires, as when Lyndon B. Johnson decided to mend bridges with poet Robert Lowell, an anti–Vietnam War protestor. After having his invitation to a White House Festival of the Arts turned down by Lowell, Johnson publicly declared his regret. After all, he commented, he was an admirer of Lowell's poetry, particularly lines like 'For the world which seems to lie out before us like a land of dreams,' unknowingly citing the epigraph to Lowell's *The Mills of the Kavanaughs*, which was from Matthew Arnold's 'Dover Beach' (Hamilton 326). (Surely a presidential speech-writer lost a job that day.) Generally, though, political celebrities have more skilfully wielded the power to confer stardom in the literary realm. That an American president had the power to so elevate a Canadian author, however, is cause for rueful meditation over the ironies of literary stardom in Canada.

To adduce a further irony, Leacock has also been recognized as one of the first celebrated literary figures in Canada to make

a conscious decision to pursue fame within Canada. Notwith-
standing his lecture tours, which could rarely be extensive,
because of his teaching commitments at McGill, Leacock
tended to pursue his fame from a Canadian vantage point,
unlike Johnson, for whom British publication and touring were
so important, or writers such as Gilbert Parker or Mazo de la
Roche, who settled for some time in Britain and pursued their
careers from the imperial metropolis. Leacock, then, would
seem to be a likely hero for later cultural nationalists in Canada.
Still, critics of his career have, more often than not, wondered if
his very commitment to working in Canada dampened the lus-
tre of his international celebrity. Albert and Theresa Moritz, in
their biography of Leacock, for example, praise him for his
commitment to 'home' markets: 'Leacock was one of those who
did not move to New York or London to find better markets or
to participate in the busy literary life of an important publishing
center' (77). Instead, they argue, Leacock was probably
inspired by the examples of Lucy Maud Montgomery and Ralph
Connor, who were able to pursue literary fame internationally
without actually leaving Canada (131). And yet, their praise
soon turns to doubt, and in their conclusion, which reads more
like an *apologia pro vita sua* than a summation of achievement,
they muse that Leacock's 'world reputation may well have been
limited by his decision to stay in Canada' (327). In the by now
classic Canadian celebrity double bind, Leacock could not win:
stay and be criticized for not attaining full-blown international
fame, or leave and be accused of turning your back on your
national culture.

Although slowly and at the instigation of our neighbours to
the south, Canada has memorialized Leacock as a celebrity in a
number of media. Since 1947, the Stephen Leacock Association, which oversees the running of the Orillia house, super-
vises the awarding of the annual Leacock Medal for Humour
(Legate 254). Past winners include Mordecai Richler, W.O.
Mitchell, and Roch Carrier. Like Pauline Johnson, Leacock has
also appeared on a Canadian stamp, in 1969, the centenary of
his birth (Moritz and Moritz 329). There is a Stephen Leacock

Public School and a Stephen Leacock Collegiate Institute in Ontario. The sculptor Esther Wertheimer has created a bronze bust of Leacock (Wertheimer). Actors Neil Ross and Aaron Duncan perform a two-man show based on a selection of Leacock stories 'in Monty Python style,' as one web site for Canada Book Day helpfully informs us ('Celebrate Canada Day'). Every summer in Orillia, the town capitalizes on its connections with Leacock by staging a one-week Laugh with Leacock Festival, complete with readings by humorists and a re-enactment of the Mad Hatter's Tea Party from *Alice in Wonderland,* a book much loved by Leacock. There are on-line chat rooms and message boards dedicated to Leacock ('Stephen Leacock'), a fact that Leacock himself, could he have been transported to the digital age, would have found immensely amusing and worthy of satire. And, in what surely must be the ultimate in celebrity memorialization, in July 1970, a 10,200-foot peak in the Yukon Territories was named Mount Leacock (Legate 254). It all sounds like a zany selection from *Literary Lapses.*

Of the 'many monuments' (Moritz and Moritz 329) to Leacock, however, the one that seems most strongly connected to the celebrity aura of the man himself is his former home on Orillia's Brewery Bay. Like the fame of Leacock himself, however, the story of the Leacock home is full of tensions and ironies. The home was declared a national historic monument on 5 July 1958, fourteen years after Leacock's death. (His son, Stephen Leacock Jr, was the owner during the intervening years.) Unfortunately, the land was sold in a couple of chunks, and one of the owners of the land adjacent to the town's portion wanted to construct a subdivision that would have significantly damaged the potential of the heritage site (Janus Museum Consultants 6–7). In the late 1960s a firm of museum consultants was hired to develop an overall plan for the Leacock House, and in 1968 the home's designation was upgraded to a national historical site. However, even in 1992, the journalist Heather Kirk wrote in *Books in Canada* that the threat of inappropriate development remained, with a private company wanting to construct a 410-unit seniors' development – 'Leacock Point' – on one portion of the original property. Over the years, concerns grew over the manuscripts and archives housed at the Leacock property, since the nearby construction of condominiums and model homes brought harmful dust and blowing dirt into the premises. Conditions subsequently improved, thanks to the intervention of the Historic Sites and Monuments Board and Parks Canada, and Orillia has reaped the benefits of increased summer tourism to the area. The site is now thriving and boasts the usual accoutrements of a national historical site – lecture space, exhibition galleries, a café, and a shop – but a nagging question remains: does the troubled history of the Leacock Home in Orillia signal an ambivalence about a once-unquestionable Canadian literary celebrity?

I think that it does, and that Leacock's fame is every bit as ambivalent as James Doyle suggests in the opening sentence of his 1992 biography: 'Stephen Leacock, one of Canada's best-known and most prolific writers, has been the subject of a great deal of biographical and critical attention and yet he is still frequently misrepresented, misunderstood, or forgotten' (13). I believe that the ambivalence surrounding Leacock's fame was present from the beginning, no matter how successful his many books were in the early decades of the twentieth century. Like Pauline Johnson, Leacock was torn by the competing claims of literary prestige and popularity, a difficult thing to believe about a writer whose aims seemed so unambiguously popular: to make people laugh. Given the wild success of his 1921 tour of Britain, he could have given up his teaching post at McGill and toured as Johnson had done to support herself. Although Johnson certainly had not made a lavish living, and, in fact, died in straitened financial circumstances, Leacock would have had considerable income from his best-selling books to count upon as well, if he had decided to make his living on tour. Still, Leacock retained his academic position until he was forcibly retired in 1936. He continued his work partly for financial reasons – since he was notoriously careful with money and loathe to let any source of income elude him – but also for reasons of prestige. He enjoyed the status that being a professor of economics at McGill brought him (Doyle 51–2), and he wanted to combine that cultural capital with the other, more frankly economic forms of capital that his appeal to a mass audience brought him. Indeed, writing brought him an income that ranged from four to eight times his academic salary (Curry 'Introducton' 9). Even so, the relationship between these types of capital in Leacock's career is not as cut-and-dried as this figure might suggest; the book that earned Leacock the most money by far was his economics textbook, *Elements of Political Science*, which was translated into nineteen languages (Staines 1).

Nevertheless, the decision to keep a hand in both scholarly and popular fields of production may have complicated readerly responses to Leacock's work. Ralph Curry argues that because Leacock 'retained his professorship at McGill University in Political Economy, there has been a kind of silent conspiracy among critics and readers to consider Stephen Leacock a gifted amateur' ('Introduction' 9). Of course, nothing of the sort befell the literary reputation of William Carlos Williams or Wallace Stevens, doctor and insurance man respectively, but they were working in a literary genre – poetry – that ensured their commitment to small-scale cultural production. As a result, the dissonance between their highly respected professional careers and their writings – often thought to be great, particularly in the case of Stevens – may be less jarring than between Leacock's elite professorial status and his role as genial, populist funnyman.

Critics who tend to rank literary genres hierarchically are particularly prone to see Leacock as an underachiever. In a number of his publications on Leacock, Donald Cameron radically questions Leacock's status as a literary star and, instead, paints him as a failure: 'By any reasonable standard Stephen Leacock was an immense success,' he writes in *Faces of Leacock*. 'Yet judged by the highest standards he failed. He had the talent to do far greater work than he did' (155). Cameron's opposition between 'any reasonable standard' and 'the highest standards' discloses the clash of Bourdieu's fields of cultural production. The 'reasonable standard' is that of mass cultural production –

the standard of money – but Cameron's coy reference to 'the highest standard' reveals that he clearly believes in the existence of a transcendent realm of cultural value that is exclusive, limited to the few high priests of culture. In an article that he published the same year as *Faces of Leacock*, Cameron offers more detail about these competing standards and cultural realms: 'By almost every index,' he writes, 'Leacock was enormously successful.' This garden-variety 'index' involves money, 'awards and literary degrees' ('Stephen Leacock' 15), but another index is waiting in the wings. Again, Cameron makes his claim that Leacock 'could have done much more' (ibid.). But what is 'much more,' and what sort of superior index does it imply? For Cameron, it entails a different, more upscale choice of literary genre: 'In all, it seems to me that Stephen Leacock could and should have written novels' (ibid.). The novel, the genre that spawned mid-twentieth-century Leavisian theories of a great tradition of literature, turns out to be Cameron's *sine qua non* of literary success. So if, as James Doyle notes, Leacock's 'considerable financial success was not accompanied by literary prizes or other distinctions' (70), there may be an institutional reason. Writers of mass-marketed comic prose tend not to be favoured for markers of literary distinction. That is why the Leacock Medal for Humour was instituted. It remains, however, a populist award, given only a fraction of the attention the publishing industry pays to more prestigious prizes such as the Booker, the Governor-General's Award, or the Whitbread, awards that may be granted to comic writing that is less populist in nature. So, ironically, the award that bears Leacock's name in tribute to his literary celebrity embodies the tensions and contradictions of that celebrity: the tug of war between prestige and popularity.

In addition to this struggle, which is common to Leacock, Johnson, and other literary celebrities of their period and ours, Leacock underwent a conflict between older and newer modes of literary fame. He relied upon certain older markers of literary fame and was both tempted and repelled by newer manifestations of literary celebrity in Canada. In lecturing, as Leacock did extensively in and around Montreal, and less often on tour, he was following in the footsteps of one of the major literary celebrities of the previous century: Charles Dickens. Still, as Albert and Theresa Moritz point out, he did not 'choose to follow up on his new-found fame' after his triumphant speaking tour of 1921 by undertaking the sorts of exhausting tours that form part of the celebrity personas of Dickens and, later, Oscar Wilde, and Dylan Thomas. In this respect, Leacock intervened in this celebrity ritual and tailored it to meet his needs; he spoke extensively in front of various public groups in Canada, but when the pace threatened his privacy or his much-prized life as a professor, he retreated to his Orillia home, purchased in 1908.

The years during which Leacock attained fame marked the crossroads of newer technologies and ways of promoting literary celebrities, and he clearly negotiated with those newer forms as actively as he did with the older ones. For instance, he was one of the first generation of Canadian writers to obtain an agent, Paul Reynolds of New York, who represented Leacock until the writer's death in 1944. As Clarence Karr points out, literary agents 'began in the 1890s to serve as brokers between authors and publishers,' but many of the authors of Leacock's time, such as L.M. Montgomery and Ralph Connor, did not put their business affairs in the hands of an agent until relatively late in their careers, to their financial detriment (77). In this respect, Leacock was most forward looking. Similarly, as one of the founding members of the Canadian Authors Association, Leacock was at the vanguard of a new, increasingly professionalized Canadian writing community, lobbying Ottawa for improvements in Canadian copyright law, for example (Doyle 52).

In addition to the new professionalization, Leacock also showed himself enthusiastic about writers' engagement with new media, most notably film and radio, though he had varying degrees of personal success in these areas. As Ralph Curry has noted, 'Stephen Leacock was much more heavily involved in these endeavours [radio, television, cinema] than is generally supposed.' Indeed, Curry muses, he 'may well have been the first significant author [in Canada, presumably] for whom these

media were "important"' ('Leacock' 23). Leacock was certainly
enthusiastic about cinema – both the possibilities of the
medium and, frankly, the star cachet attached to Hollywood.
According to his niece, Elizabeth Kimball, Leacock '*knew other
rich, famous people.* People like Mary Pickford and Doug Fairbanks, Charlie Chaplin, Booth Tarkington, and other such glit-
tering personalities, who were very much part of the smart
scene in the thirties and forties' (27). We know that Leacock
was so smitten with his Hollywood connections that he hastened
to invite the newly married Douglas Fairbanks and Mary Pickford to his home in Montreal and was nervously taken up with
preparations for their august arrival. Legate concludes that Leacock was star-struck: 'The professor courted the stage and anybody on it' and 'the same applied to the world of motion
pictures' (136). Apart from his adulation of film celebrities,
however, Leacock remained oddly detached from the industry.
Apparently he would remark to anyone that a number of his
works would have suited the medium, and that seems obviously
to be the case, but, as Albert and Theresa Moritz conclude,
despite his 'persistent interest in film' in his later years, 'it is
clear that Leacock only dabbled with the industry at long-range
and hoped for a lucky strike' (303).

   This was not true of radio. Leacock did involve himself in a
number of radio adaptations of his works, and he even experimented, in 1934, as a radio broadcaster of some of his humorous sketches. These shows failed, however, to win an audience,
probably because his method of delivery, perfected upon the
lecture stage, did not translate well to radio. This was particularly true of Leacock's trademark tendency to chuckle as he told
his stories. To a radio audience, this might seem odd or even
irritating (Curry, 'Leacock' 24–5; Doyle 66). So it remains somewhat of a mystery why Leacock invested so much time in radio
but not in the movies, a medium that fascinated him and that
would seem much better equipped to accommodate his work,
given the considerable appetite of early movie audiences for the
humour of Chaplin or Keaton. I would suggest that Leacock,
like other writers of his day, did not feel entirely comfortable

with the industry, in spite of his celebrity infatuation. Many writers of the period, as Clarence Karr has shown, were uncomfortable with the business aspects of movie making and did not know quite how to go about dealing with movie contracts (172). On the face of it, this does not seem to apply to Leacock, since he wrote about these matters in many letters dealing with the filmic possibilities of his works (Moritz and Moritz 303). His reluctance remains, to my mind, one of the mysteries of Leacock's celebrity, but, for whatever reason, his ambivalence about newer technologies of celebrity comes to the fore in this issue of his relationship with Hollywood.

Another, related aspect of Hollywood-style celebrity that I believe Leacock struggled with and never felt comfortable about, was the growing willingness of stars, whether filmic or literary, to disclose details of their private lives. Neal Gabler argues that this tendency has grown to such an extent in present-day culture that stars' life narratives or 'lifies' become valued over their art. This eventuality would clearly have been anathema to Leacock. As numerous critics and biographers have noticed, Leacock was an extremely private man and therefore something of an enigma, and so he remains, essentially, today. Leacock's family life 'was perhaps the subject most closed from public view' (Moritz and Moritz 214), and, furthermore, in the years since his death, no Leacock scholar 'has done much to get behind Leacock's mask regarding family matters' (Lucas 124). Leaving aside the whole theoretical issue of whether biographers ever do glimpse anything besides masks, it is true that biographical speculation about Leacock's private realm continues apace. Although his works have not spawned a great deal of critical inquiry in recent years, the biographies keep on appearing, a testimony to the continuing fascination with this very public but reticent man. In addition to the various print biographies, there has also been an instalment of CBC's biography program *Life and Times* devoted to Leacock in 2000. As the CBC Web site makes clear, the program, too, traded on the idea that Leacock was a man of masks; Leacock was 'a man burdened in ways that were deeply hidden.'

During his lifetime, Leacock strongly resisted any disclosure of his private life, and in this way showed himself to be deeply ambivalent about the form of celebrity discourse and culture – the 'lifie' – that was beginning to gain ascendancy. Leacock's characteristic interview technique has been described as an uneasy dance of self-dramatization and reticence: 'He preferred to spin yarns of his own choosing and reveal himself in that way rather than provide direct answers to questions about his private life or to be treated as an enigma suitable for dissection' (Moritz and Moritz 8). Ironically, of course, the latter impression of Leacock has prevailed among his biographers, and they have contented themselves with representing the panoply of personas that Leacock would assume, in turn, rather than discovering and laying bare some sort of underlying grand biographical narrative. As even recent biographers must admit, the 'lack of evidence about Leacock's intimacies indicates that he was a man who could keep the most private side of his life to himself' (Doyle 61) – a daunting candidate for any biographer to take on. Rather than reading this reluctance in purely personal, idiosyncratic terms, however, I read Leacock's reticence as evidence of a conflict in his career between older and newer modes of fame circulating and jostling for ascendancy in his time. The public lecturer, like the vaudevillian, was in the process of ceding cultural authority to the radio broadcaster and the film star, and Stephen Leacock, Dickensian humorist, was both attracted to and repelled by the mass-technology successors he saw stepping onto the celebrity stage.

Some decades later, a modern Canadian novelist, Mordecai Richler, would lump Leacock's name along with that of another early-twentieth-century Canadian literary celebrity in his own personal hall of shame: 'If the literary house is haunted,' a determinedly cosmopolitan Richler once remarked of his Canadian homeland, 'it's only by the amiable Leacock, the dispensable de la Roche.' Mazo de la Roche, author of the literary marathon that was the Jalna series, was an unquestioned literary star of the twenties and thirties, but she would prove to be, without question, the dispensable member of the early celebrity quartet I examine here. Far from haunting the literary house, de la Roche seemed, for a while, to have abandoned it. In 1995, de la Roche scholar Ruth Panofsky observed that 'de la Roche's achievement as a popular author and her writing and publishing career have been largely overlooked by literary scholars' ('Don't Let Me!' 171). In recent years, Panofsky herself has contributed to the revival of interest in de la Roche, along with other scholars such as Joan Givner, Daniel Bratton, and Faye Hammill, but for the most part, the de la Roche room in the literary house has seen little traffic.

In her heyday, however, she was the object of her fans' fascinated gaze, as is evident in novelist and playwright Timothy Findley's recollection of his childhood sighting of de la Roche: 'I had seen Mazo once, on the street in Toronto. And this had some importance. Mazo was an icon. My mother and I were walking on Bloor Street, near where the Ladies' Club used to be, and a big black car with a chauffeur stopped and Mazo was let out and she looked something like the character actress in the movies – Edna May Oliver – tall, angular, not pretty. But she had presence – and she had style and absolute grace. My mother said to me – I was still a child – "Look and remember this. That is Mazo de la Roche!" As though one were seeing God' (Bratton 159). This passage betrays many of the recognizable trademarks of fan discourse: the thunderous shock experienced when the realms of the celebrity and of the ordinary citizen intersect; the elevation of the celebrity through comparisons with other stars, in this case a star sanctified and validated by Hollywood; the notion of the celebrity as endowed with special graces that set her apart; the conspicuous consumption and 'lifestyle' of the star; and the overwhelming experience of deistic visitation.

Fame Mazo de la Roche certainly had, and to a degree that many twenty-first-century observers might find surprising to consider, used as we are to thinking of earlier Canadian writers as, somehow, more homespun or unaffected by the workings of celebrity. Yet, following 'the success of *Jalna* she became a celebrity, honored in Canada and abroad' (Daymond 110). When she won the coveted $10,000 Atlantic Monthly Prize for fiction with *Jalna* in 1927, she was caught up in a whirlwind of publicity, celebration, and public life that sounds uncannily like the fate of contemporary writers who find themselves honoured by a Booker Prize or a nod from Oprah Winfrey's book club. Toronto gave a grand banquet in her honour. The women of Toronto honoured her at Casa Loma, and de la Roche became, she believed, the first woman to be honoured by a banquet at the Toronto Arts and Letters Club (Panofsky, 'At Odds' 60; de la Roche 218). As de la Roche later recalled, 'newspaper reporters crowded into our living-room; there were interviews and articles. Telegrams, flowers, letters of congratulation deluged us' (217).

As was the case with Pauline Johnson, this scenario of sudden fame managed to obscure public awareness of de la Roche's apprenticeship, and both the writer and her publishers colluded in the obfuscation in order to stoke the fires of celebrity. Though some critics still refer to de la Roche as 'a virtually unknown writer' who 'shot overnight to world fame and fortune' (Givner, 'Deciphering' 194, *The Hidden Life* 1), the truth is somewhat more complicated, as Ruth Panofsky and others have shown. De la Roche was well known to the staff of the *Atlantic Monthly*, since they had previously published two of her stories, and she had become friendly with its editor, Ellery Sedgwick, thirteen years prior to her 'overnight success.' The *Atlantic Monthly* sought to suppress these facts in all its promotion of de la Roche and *Jalna* in 1927 (Panofsky, 'At Odds' 60), presumably to work readers up into a frenzy of curiosity about this new literary star, the better to persuade them to buy her book. The *Atlantic Monthly* proved itself eager to embrace a fundamental aspect of the relatively new Hollywood marketing strategy: the promotion of the new face, the 'it girl' of the moment.

Mazo de la Roche's fame was a complicated construction, and nowhere is this more in evidence than in her own complex and canny representations of it. When she came to write her notoriously impressionistic and creative memoirs in 1957, she was more than willing to dramatize herself as a victim of the crass, intrusive forces of stardom: 'I was photographed on the deck surrounded by sixteen men in the book business. I still have the photograph, in which, wearing a great bunch of violets, I look dreadfully like a movie star. That night, casting myself on my berth completely exhausted, I burst into tears. I thought I knew what movie stars felt when they took an overdose of sleeping tablets and ended all publicity' (237). Daniel Bratton has speculated that some of the fictional experiences of Finch Whiteoak, the sensitive artist figure in the Jalna novels (based, apparently, on the poet Robert Finch), reflect de la Roche's own conflicting responses to literary fame: 'Finch Whiteoak's response to inheriting his grandmother's legacy in *Whiteoaks of Jalna* clearly expresses the conflicting emotions that Mazo felt on the heels of her own stunning success' (87). His fluctuating reactions to being on stage, 'between wanting to be swallowed by the earth and feeling he's walking on air,' similarly 'provide an analogue to what Mazo must have experienced in the face of all these public appearances' (97). Of course, as with any such biographical speculation, it is impossible to know, but the notion of the would-be aristocrat Mazo de la Roche embodying her fame as a family inheritance or as a high-art performance is suggestive. These would be ways for de la Roche to justify, in class terms, her achievement of fame, as she does in the portrait of herself as a sensitive, beleaguered woman who collapses, weeping, in her berth, a victim of the indignity of crass fame. That crassness is rather humorously figured in the vision of de la Roche, wearing her violets, surrounded by sixteen publishing men – a parody of a 1930s musical production number, in which the bedecked starlet, surrounded by tuxedoed dancing men, struts her stuff. For a woman of de la Roche's imagined class pretensions, such a fate seems worth than death – even a Hollywood-style barbiturate binge.

Whether she approved of its class overtones or not, de la Roche's fame was in the vanguard of new developments in literary celebrity in Canada. In particular, her career, more than those of Leacock, Johnson, and Montgomery, brings into play the increasingly visible role of literary awards in this country during the first half of the twentieth century. In 1927, a decade

before the first Governor General's Awards would be handed
out, major literary awards, by definition, had their origins elsewhere, and it was still a novelty for a Canadian to win them. As a
number of critics have pointed out, however, in the media
frenzy that erupted with the announcement that de la Roche
had won the Atlantic Monthly Prize, the precedent of one earlier prize-winning Canadian woman writer was largely forgotten: Martha Ostenso, who two years previously won the $13,500
prize awarded by the American periodical *Pictorial Review*, in
partnership with the Famous Players–Lasky Corporation and
Dodd-Mead publishers, for her first novel, *Wild Geese* (Hambleton, *Mazo* 45). As Joan Givner speculates, the publicity surrounding de la Roche's prize was greater because Ostenso 'had
been born in Norway and had had to claim American citizenship in order to be eligible for the prize' (*Hidden Life* 121),
since it could be awarded only to first novels by American citizens. Because Ostenso immigrated at the age of two and lived
with her family in Minnesota and North Dakota before moving
to Manitoba, her initial immigration to the United States quali-
fied her for the prize. So, Givner intimates, the construction of
nationality that allowed fans of de la Roche to celebrate a landmark Canadian achievement was predicated upon an implicit
disenfranchisement of Ostenso as not *really* a Canadian writer.
This Canadianization of de la Roche would eventually attract its
own irony, as, with every Jalna installment, Canadian critics
would complain that the series was less and less Canadian in
content, more and more pseudo-Galsworthian. More recently,
Faye Hammill has observed that de la Roche's novel received a
warmer reception in Canada than Ostenso's because its anti-
American, pro-British flavour was preferable to Ostenso's
apparent continentalism. This would appear to confirm Nick
Mount's observations about the excision of émigré authors
from the evolving narrative of Canadian literature during the
opening decades of the twentieth century. A further irony:
Canadian literati were eager to celebrate a woman born Maisie
Roche in Newmarket, Ontario, who deliberately constructed a
pseudo-European persona for herself as 'Mazo de la Roche.'

According to prevailing constructions of Canadian nationality as English, that was more Canadian than Martha Ostenso could ever, apparently, hope to be.

As the years went on, this fraught relationship between nationality and literary achievement continued to plague de la Roche. For her, as for Pauline Johnson, fame allowed the opportunity to travel, but that travel, in turn, seemed to jeopardize her status as an exemplary Canadian author. In the wake of the Atlantic Monthly Prize, travel was clearly the first priority for de la Roche and her lover, Caroline Clement. In her memoirs, *Ringing the Changes,* de la Roche relates the discussion that she and Clement had when it became clear that she had won the prestigious prize: 'After a little I said, "It is a large prize I have won." "Yes, it is large," she agreed. "Now we can travel"' (215). Originally planning to take a trip around the world, the two women, on the advice of Professor Pelham Edgar of the University of Toronto, agreed on an Italian tour before settling in England in the thirties. It was at this point in her career that critics in Canada began to grumble about de la Roche's later Jalna novels. Implicit in that critical unhappiness was the suspicion that de la Roche had, by setting up house in England, abandoned the Canadianness that had been conferred upon her with the winning of the Atlantic Monthly Prize. By the time she returned, in 1939, the impression of her world as one manufactured elsewhere, in England, was firmly established among critics, and, as interest in promoting Canadian content grew in the 1950s, her cultural capital in the developing discourse of Canadian literary nationalism declined dramatically. The manifold ironies of nationality and prize winning that animated the career of Mazo de la Roche continue into the present day, as the career of Pulitzer Prize – winning Canadian writer Carol Shields plainly gives evidence.

De la Roche continued to covet literary awards, though she won fewer of them as her status as a high-art novelist declined after the initial success of *Jalna* and she turned, more and more, to the demands of large-scale cultural production – namely, pleasing her legions of readers. Still, she was bitterly disappointed in the 1940s to have been told by a judge for the recently created Governor General's Awards that she would likely win the award, only to discover that it was given to another writer in the final event (Hambleton, *Mazo* 55). De la Roche never did win the Governor General's Award, and Joan Givner argues that her bitter disappointment about this perceived home-ground snub caused her to pursue the ultimate international literary award: the Nobel Prize for Literature. In the forties and fifties, she approached her various publishers, urging them to nominate her for the Nobel (Givner, *Hidden Life* 198–200). Several were clearly embarrassed by her request, and none responded with much enthusiasm, so de la Roche's campaign never gained any momentum. It is as though de la Roche, having been launched into the world of literary celebrity by the force of an international prize, vainly hoped for another, much more sensational prize to compensate for the cooling of critical responses to her Jalna books and to re-establish her rightful place in the celebrity firmament, where she felt she so rightfully belonged.

If there was one aspect of de la Roche's career that never cooled, however, it was her financial success. The Atlantic Monthly Prize of $10,000, a substantial amount of money in 1927, sparked greater earnings, as the *New York Times*, in its announcement of the award, rightly predicted it would: 'As a prize novel brought out under such circumstances is almost certain to become a best seller, Miss de la Roche stands to realize a substantial fortune' ('Toronto Woman' 23). This she did, and although critical opinion about her work steadily declined throughout the thirties, forties, and, most disastrously, the fifties, her sales figures continued buoyant. The Jalna series sold more than eleven million copies during de la Roche's lifetime, and ran to 193 English editions and 92 editions in other languages (Hambleton, *Mazo* 50; Daymond 108). Even as publishers became concerned about the literary quality of some of the sequels, and risked de la Roche's wrath by asking for revisions, they could not deny the selling power of her books. As Edward Weeks, de la Roche's editor at the Atlantic affiliate Little, Brown and Company, reassured her on the publication of *Young Renny* in 1934, 'An advance sale (with no copies on consignment!) of 22,000 is something to write home about. We have printed 30,000 copies altogether to make sure that we had a surplus for the reorders which are now coming in on the footsteps of the highly favorable reviews' (qtd. Panofsky 'Don't Let Me!' 181). For any publisher struggling during the years of the Depression, having Mazo de la Roche on one's list must have seemed the equivalent of having a novel chosen for Oprah Winfrey's book club: it meant an absolute guarantee of enormous sales. De la Roche was fully cognizant of her power, and, as Panofsky has shown in careful detail, she used her considerable sales power over her publishers on any number of occasions, to win concessions or better financial arrangements from them ('Don't Let Me!'). No wonder that a few years after her death, one of her English publishers recollected that de la Roche was 'a goldmine to anybody who has ever had anything to do with her' (Hambleton *Mazo* 7, 53).

Even if, as Ronald Hambleton argues, de la Roche's exact earnings 'cannot be exactly stated' (*Mazo* 54), it is certain that they allowed her to enjoy an opulent lifestyle, and that she lost no time in doing so after she won the Atlantic Monthly Prize. She seems, on the surface, to have been minimally conflicted about her fame and success, but, in reality, she seems to have basked in it. More than other Canadian literary stars of her day, de la Roche constructed a literary celebrity lifestyle for herself, with none of the apologies, none of the stereotypically Canadian embarrassment or self-effacement that Karr perceives in his popular authors. Dennis Duffy refers to it as an 'opulent lifestyle ... that made possible shifts between English country houses and Ontario mansions' (103). In fact, Joan Givner reveals that de le Roche added an epigraph on bell ringing to her memoirs, *Ringing the Changes*, 'lest readers, aware of her wealth, should associate her title with a cash register' ('Deciphering' 198). But deny it or not, the cash register did ring for Mazo de la Roche, and her consumption of the material fruits of her success was nothing if not conspicuous.

For all that de la Roche feigned to abhor the publicity that accompanied her fame, she was also desirous of it and adept at gaining it without actually appearing to do so. She claimed throughout her career that publicity destroyed her privacy, and to some extent this was undoubtedly true. Ronald Hambleton writes of the insatiable public thirst for details of de la Roche's life that arose after she won her first major prize; interviewers and fans wanted to know 'everything: physical description of the author, her favourite foods, her hobbies and recreations – everything' (*Mazo* 43). In the days and months following her spectacular win, de la Roche and Caroline Clement made decisions about how much and what sort of information to release to the public, although, as Hambleton bemusedly notes, de la Roche tended to forget such agreements in a public moment of fancy, when she would inadvertently utter some unguarded tidbit that was not part of the agreement, or not even close to verifiable truth (*Mazo* 43–4). Still, if Mazo could lead the media astray, it is also true that the media could, on occasion, play fast and loose with her persona and with the ethics of journalism. On one occasion, de la Roche left the room during an interview to find a particular document, and she returned to find the journalist blithely examining the private contents of her desk (Hambleton, *The Secret* 95). As early as 1923, after the publication of her novel *Delight*, de la Roche was revolted to read, in *Canadian Bookman*, a series of purple prose passages about her cottage in Clarkson, Ontario, attributed to her by a journalist who interviewed her there. De la Roche used the space of her scrapbook to gain final authorial control over this irresponsible journalism; over a particularly purplish passage, de la Roche scribbled, 'My god! Can such things be!' (Hambleton, *Mazo* 116). As the experiences of other literary celebrities such as Lucy Maud Montgomery amply show, such things definitely *were*, in the world of early twentieth-century Canadian journalism, and authors did not yet have the sorts of privacy rights that allowed them to police misquotation and misrepresentation, as, by the legal philosophy of the time, celebrities had ceded privacy rights in becoming public persons.

At the same time, Mazo de la Roche could make much of her lack of privacy precisely in order to reinforce her image as a literary icon. Here is where scholars of her work and career take divergent paths, some expressing undiluted sympathy for her loss of privacy as an internationally famous author, and others maintaining a more sceptical stance. Panofsky takes the former position, repeatedly referring to de la Roche's 'intense dislike of publicity throughout her life' ('At Odds' 61). Givner similarly assumes that de la Roche 'shunned publicity' ('Deciphering' 194) and even that her 'dislike for publicity amounted to an obsession' (*Hidden Life* 2). Such an observation contains the seeds of its own interrogation, however. De la Roche did, indeed, have an obsession with privacy, but it was one that, paradoxically, fed her audience's desire for information. This might be called the Greta Garbo effect or, to evoke a more literary example, the Thomas Pynchon syndrome.

De la Roche was not, for example, so averse to promotion and publicity that she refrained from celebrity endorsement. As Nina M. Ray has shown, one of the most prominently featured writers in celebrity endorsements of consumer products was Ernest Hemingway, both during his life and, especially, after his death (77). De la Roche, whose celebrity image as a refined, upper-class Anglophile was the opposite of the tough American he-man persona embodied by Hemingway, nevertheless ended up endorsing one of the same products: the Parker 51 pen. Below a smiling studio portrait of de la Roche, her testimonial ran: 'In many countries and at all times ... I have found my Parker pen a faithful friend. If it is possible to improve anything so excellent the new 51 has done just that' (Hambleton, *Secret* 144). So much for the reclusive de la Roche, stung by the crass intrusions of publicity; rather, she shared marketing assignments with America's ultimate literary logo: Papa Hemingway.

De la Roche was also so taken with her celebrity status that she carefully preserved much of the voluminous fan mail that she received during the course of her long career. Ten boxes of her correspondence survive in the Thomas Fisher Rare Book Library at the University of Toronto, and fan mail makes up the bulk of her collection there. In the first two years after de la Roche won the Atlantic Monthly Prize, she received from one to twelve letters every day (Hambleton, *Mazo* 53). As the years went on, no matter how much critics panned the later Jalna installments, a steady flow of fan mail came her way, care of her various publishers. During the Second World War for example, she received a great deal of fan mail from Europe (Duffy 103). As Hambleton points out, this enormous fan correspondence necessitated that for de la Roche, like 'most successful people – part of every day had to be given over to correspondence with people she knew only by name' (*Mazo de la Roche* 53). Currently, more often than not, writers who receive this amount of fan mail, including Margaret Atwood, need to hire assistants to help them deal with it, or all private time given over to writing would become engulfed by this most public of duties. Caroline Clement did, in a sense, fulfill some of this role for de la Roche, but much of the responsibility for answering the fan mail rested with de la Roche herself.

This is the sort of public duty that might well move a celebrity writer to bemoan her loss of privacy, and de la Roche would seem a likely candidate to do so, but this was not the way she responded to her fan mail. On the contrary, she found a great deal of pleasure in it and, more than pleasure, justification. As Lovat Dickson, one of her editors, remarked of de la Roche's 'absolutely enormous' fan mail, 'She liked those sorts of tributes' (Panofsky, 'At Odds' 65). 'All authors like to feel that they are communicating with their readers, and she liked the tributes and the fan mail; she liked watching her audience grow, and all the signals of success pleased her – surely it made her feel that what she was doing was giving wide pleasure' (Hambleton, *Mazo* 53–4). The word 'tribute,' repeatedly used by Dickson, with its connotations of obligatory genuflection before one's betters, seems particularly suited to de la Roche's class pretensions. Panofsky, who has studied de la Roche's fan mail in the most detail, persuasively argues that it acted as a compensation for the elite literary recognition that did not, on the whole, come de la Roche's way after the first blush of her prize-winning success

('At Odds' 64–5). Fans responded positively 'to exactly those aspects of *Jalna* that reviewers found offensive' (ibid. 68), and that fact would have comforted de la Roche as she faced increasingly hostile reviews. De la Roche's fan mail, then, tended to stroke an ego that was frequently ruffled by the loss of institutionalized literary esteem or cultural capital. But in seeking this solace, de la Roche was also embracing an aspect of celebrity culture that was at odds with her avowed conservative dislike of all such déclassé forms of public display. Like Leacock, she was torn between various manifestations of celebrity culture, but the primary antagonism in her case was between class and ego.

Similarly, de la Roche's legendary tendency to fabricate details of her past, which might be read as evidence of her determination to protect the actual details of her private life, was actually an attempt to present a more dashing image to her public: Mazo de la Roche, aristocratic descendant of a French rebel guillotined in the revolution, rather than Maisie Roche from a lower-middle-class family in southern Ontario. As Daniel Bratton has remarked, we 'all, of course, devise our own narratives, but Mazo was in a league of her own, up there with Jay Gatsby' (14). In the wake of her supposedly overnight success, de la Roche was asked for biographical information by *Atlantic Monthly* for use in publicity, and either she, Caroline Clement, or the two women working in tandem (critics are unsure) concocted a whimsical web of lies and half-lies that does rival Jay Gatsby's naive self-reinvention. In her later autobiography, de la Roche disingenuously claimed that 'Caroline filled in the form as best she could, with only a few mistakes' (217), an account of the event that Bratton characterizes as an 'amusing' instance of de la Roche's 'penchant for exaggeration and out and out lying' (15). These questionnaire responses included the infamous tale of the guillotined French ancestor, as well as the false information that de le Roche's education was 'mostly private, with an erratic dash or two into the University of Toronto' (Givner, *Hidden Life* 126). The university's registrar kept no records of these erratic dashes, and de la Roche came to regret having given in to the temptation to falsify her educational record. What's more, her publishers were surprised, not to say seized with consternation, at her responses to their questionnaire. The *Atlantic Monthly* people knew, or thought they knew, that de la Roche had been in great need of money to support herself and her writing during the lengthy apprenticeship that she had with the magazine and its editor, and they had, on occasion, taken steps to assist the indigent author. Yet the completed questionnaire painted a picture of de la Roche as an old Toronto aristocrat who was anything but concerned over filthy lucre. As one editor warmly exclaimed to a colleague in an in-house memo, 'I think we've been worrying unduly about her poverty – these facts do not corroborate our surmises!' (qtd. Givner, *Hidden Life* 127). Once again, the trappings of instant success clashed with the lived experience of a literary apprenticeship.

However much de la Roche regretted some of her rasher moments of self-aggrandizing fabrication, she continued to falsify many biographical details for the rest of her life. Critics have tried to account for her compulsive lying by arguing that it was a response to overly intrusive publicity (Givner) or an attempt to hide her lower-middle-class origins, which she apparently found shameful. And although it may have owed something to both of these motives, de la Roche's penchant for fabrication also fed into an increasingly popular part of celebrity culture: the thirst for biographical legend under the guise of biographical revelation. Originally, in the earliest Hollywood films, actors were not even acknowledged as individuals, much less individuals whose private lives were the object of scrutiny, but increasingly, fans began to demand knowledge of the real lives of the Pickfords and the Fairbankses. Publicity departments obliged, creating many a narrative that was no more fantastical than many of the lies de la Roche trotted out. Initially, they were often fairy tales of the stars' happy marriages, for only later did Hollywood publicists realize that producing narratives of unhappy relationships proved just as tempting to consumers. (In fact, the way in which the press managed to construct the Pickford–Fairbanks relationship as an idealized romance, without getting caught up in the

messiness of their adultery and Fairbanks's divorce that preceded their marriage, is an amazing testimony to the sway of the
fairy-tale narrative at the time.) De la Roche, whether she realized it or not, was playing the same sort of game with her fans,
and her readers responded with increasingly fantastic specula-
tions of their own about her life. Eventually, what Dyer would call
a star image solidified; as Ronald Hambleton observes, 'by the
late 1940s the unreal impression of her that had been gradually
built up over the years became her permanent image: a shy,
somewhat embittered, wealthy literary recluse who turned out
retreads of a product that had proved to be universally marketable' (*Mazo* 7) – a Miss Havisham, old Toronto–style. Hambleton's conclusion, though, that readers, on the whole, didn't
much care about the details of de la Roche's life, that they
'basked, without curiosity about her real life, in the romantic
worlds she created' (7), seems contradicted by the wealth of
rumours that floated around her. As Givner reports, apparently
the Miss Havisham persona was all too suggestive; some fans
speculated that she, like Dickens's embittered aristocrat, had
been jilted at the altar. When de la Roche and Clement adopted
two children, rumours about their origins swirled for years: were
they illegitimate children of de la Roche's (Givner, *Hidden Life*
3)? (Sadly, de la Roche never saw fit to enlighten the children
themselves on this point.) But the ultimate fabrication was the
speculation that de la Roche was, herself, nothing more than
that: a fabrication. According to Ronald Hambleton, there was 'a
rumour that she did not exist, that the name Mazo de la Roche
was a "house name" of her publishers, and that the Whiteoak
books were turned out by a stable of obedient hacks' (*Mazo* 7–8).
Like the climax of a Jorge Luis Borges fable, the construction of
de la Roche's star persona ultimately seemed to form a dizzying
hall of mirrors, a confounding celebrity shell game that captured
the attention of her fans.

The same debate about de la Roche seems to arise again and
again, in relation to her lies, her apparent love of privacy and
hatred of publicity: was this particular manifestation of celebrity
what she wanted or what she fell victim to? In essence, this is the

question asked relentlessly about celebrity: Is this condition one of power or powerlessness? Choice or happenstance? The question applies particularly well to de la Roche's publishing format: the sequel. Most commentators see the seemingly never-ending Whiteoaks saga as a sales and marketing trap that de la Roche fell into, egged on by greedy publishers. As her former neighbour in Clarkson, Dorothy Livesay, recalled, 'I remember how the publishers then harried Mazo. They did not want her to write of the down-and-outs, the characters she knew that reminded her of Dickens, those disinherited whom she had described in *Possession* and *Delight* [the two novels predating *Jalna*]. No, she must stay with "the good thing," popular acclaim for *Jalna*, popular demand for more and more about the Whiteoaks family' (13). There is some truth in this; publishers are always keen for writers to provide them with marketable writings, but whether de la Roche's literary vocation was really to write about the 'down-and-outs' and the 'disinherited' is open to debate. In many ways, it sounds much more like Livesay's. Another writer, Timothy Findley, so agrees with Livesay about the destructiveness of the Jalna sequels that he characterizes them as a pernicious disease, and places de la Roche alongside another early Canadian literary celebrity as a fellow sufferer: 'She was limited by the expectations of her society. "Ah, you've written a book, have you. Do give us another just like it!" They sucked her in, the way they had sucked in Lucy Maud Montgomery. *Anne and Emily forever! and –* Jalna *forever too!* It was like a cancer, and it grew on Mazo like a cancer and it ate her alive' (qtd. Bratton 163). True, de la Roche did write fifteen sequels to *Jalna*, and such a literary marathon did little to advance her critical reputation, however much it filled her coffers and those of her publishers. By the time her last volume appeared in 1960, the year of her death, critical commentary was vicious. As the reviewer for the *Times Literary Supplement* sniped, 'there is nothing to make one squeamish about Miss de la Roche's seventeenth [*sic*] instalment of the Whiteoak family saga – unless one cares about literature ... The Jalna marathon has, indeed, moved outside the range of literary criteria' ('Such Darling

Dodos' 477). Panofsky argues that such an attack marks the final banishment of de la Roche from standards of the literary largely because of her status as a popular writer. I would add, however, that it is the very fact of the sequel itself – the publishing format – and the ridiculous extent to which de la Roche took it, that make the saga seem less like a literary event and more like a sporting one. The overwhelming sense is of a writer losing control of her publishing career, and, in the world of celebrity discourse in general, loss of control is cited as an all too frequent corollary of stardom.

Alone among her critics, Ruth Panofsky speculates that, instead of being enslaved to the sequel by self-interested publishers and by her readers, Mazo de la Roche embraced it as her artistic mission. This is part of Panofsky's overall argument about de la Roche becoming, increasingly, mistress of her own professional career ('Don't Let Me!'). Drawing on the voluminous correspondence among de la Roche and her publishers, and between her publishers, Panofsky has revealed that, in fact, her closest literary adviser and publisher, Hugh Eayrs, president of Macmillan Canada, secretly wanted de la Roche to call a halt to the Whiteoaks saga after the third volume, but, as he wrote to Edward Weeks of Atlantic Monthly Press / Little, Brown, 'she seems bent on it' ('Don't Let Me!' 177). Presumably, Eayrs still harboured some hopes of turning de la Roche into a canonized writer of fine literature rather than a primarily popular, best-selling one. Even though other publishers were doubtless less rarefied in their hopes for her, it still appears to be an oversimplification to say that de la Roche published sequels because her publishers pressured her to do so. It seems far more accurate to say that some of her publishers had serious doubts about the continuation of the series, but many were wary of approaching the rather testy author on this subject, lest she jump ship to another publishing house (something she routinely threatened to do), or they were sufficiently well rewarded by the profits that they shelved their private concerns. From the point of view of celebrity culture, what is revealing about this whole debate is the way in which literary stars of de la Roche's magnitude are often assumed to have no power – to be, in James Monaco's terms, 'quasars' or 'passive objects of the media' (6).

Mazo de la Roche's career dramatizes the rivalry between cultural and economic capital in literary production in a way that is much more emphatic than any of the other early Canadian literary careers I survey here. Her literary reputation travelled so dramatically from prize-winning success and the possibility of success in the arena of small-scale production to a final banishment from the very category of the literary into the fallen world of the economic. Still, it would be mistaken to plot her career as a classic rise and fall, as Desmond Pacey appeared to do when he wrote in his introduction to the New Canadian Library edition of *Delight* that, although Canadians praised *Jalna* when it appeared, they 'either condemned her work as trivial or damned it with faint praise' 'both before and since' (qtd. Hambleton, *Mazo* 168). Ronald Hambleton challenges this perception, but he does so by continuing to plot de la Roche's career on a linear path; he notes that no 'part of [Pacey's] statement is borne out by the facts'; rather, 'it is becoming apparent that Mazo de la Roche's admirers are more numerous than anyone might have supposed, although their admiration is expressed privately' (*Mazo de la Roche* 169). What Hambleton needs as part of his critical methodology is a way of speaking about competing spheres of cultural reception – the popular and the more academic – instead of assuming that critical reception is monistic. Panofsky's article 'At Odds: Reviewers and Readers of the Jalna Novels' supplies that missing methodology by tracing in some detail how de la Roche's fiction came to be vilified by the high priests of culture during the same years that it was bought, read, and celebrated by millions of private readers. She calls this situation the 'paradox of professional marginalization and popular success' (58), and it is, in Bourdieu's sociology of culture, a paradigmatic condition of the field of cultural production. This paradox was always in play in de la Roche's career, as, for instance, when her editor Edward Weeks counselled her against moving her allegiance to *Cosmopolitan*, who had just made her a persuasive offer, because her reputation as a serious novelist would no doubt suffer as a result of being associated with the popular productions of that magazine (Panofsky, 'Don't Let Me!' 176). Of course, as Panofsky points out, the irony remains that, whether she stayed with *Atlantic Monthly* or not, her reputation among critical specialists was eventually tarnished anyway. Still, that did not stop de la Roche from chasing after high-profile literary honours like the Governor General's Award or even the Nobel Prize. So, rather than providing a narrative of rise into critical acclaim and decline into popularity, her career presents us with a portrait of overlapping, competing spheres of cultural production. This is the very essence of Mazo de la Roche's stardom and, arguably, of literary celebrity in general.

The same is true of L.M. Montgomery, whose literary réclame was sparked by the publication of *Anne of Green Gables* in 1908. Like de la Roche, Montgomery was an immensely popular novelist whose critical reputation suffered during the middle years of the twentieth century. Unlike de la Roche, though, Montgomery has resurfaced, to some extent, in academic Canadian literature circles, though her status there seems still marginal, in many ways. Still, no past or present literary celebrity in Canada has had the far-reaching cultural influence that L.M. Montgomery had – and continues to have. As Carole Gerson has remarked, the 'charisma' of Montgomery and her best-known creation, *Anne of Green Gables*, 'spills far beyond the notions of value constructed by the traditional literary critic, into a dense web of cultural activity that includes romance and popular culture, national identity, provincial and international economics, and social history' ('Dragged' 146). There simply is no comparable Canadian literary persona who has filtered into the culture at large in the way that L.M. Montgomery has. Also, in the figure of Montgomery we have a particularly rich archive that helps us to understand the complexities of early-twentieth-century literary fame, because, far from being the innocent small-town Canadian literary star described by Clarence Karr, Montgomery was unusually articulate about and aware of the conditions and ironies of her celebrity.

In her contribution to the collection of essays *Making Avonlea:*

L.M. Montgomery and Popular Culture (2002), E. Holly Pike opens up Montgomery's celebrity for sustained analysis. Typically, Montgomery's celebrity has been briefly summarized, assumed, and memorialized, but it has not been closely analysed as a phenomenon in its own right, with connections to other systems of celebrity. Pike, for her part, is specifically interested in the operations of celebrity in the literary field; in particular, she explores how Montgomery's publishers 'created a suitable authorial persona to market the books ... based on the demands of mass marketing' (239). Such an analysis would seem to suggest a theory of stars being manufactured by hegemonic interests, but Pike is unwilling to depict Montgomery as merely the passive product of top-down literary marketing. As she proposes, 'Montgomery was aware of the disparity between the marketing persona and herself.' She also suggests that Montgomery 'had accepted and actively shaped her role as a celebrity,' offering as evidence the fact that Montgomery agreed to make some information about her private life available to her publishers for publicity purposes (246). I seek to open up this space for Montgomery's celebrity agency even further, probing the relationship between celebrity manufacture and celebrity agency or intervention, which I see as one of the vexed yet repressed questions in existing theories of celebrity. Going beyond Montgomery's simple agreement to participate in the commercialization of her works, I maintain that she developed a strategic and remarkably intelligent negotiation with the celebrity processes that surrounded and, in part, tried to define her.

In 1997, Masashi Matsumoto, a Japanese writer, told journalist Judy Stoffman that 'If you ask a Japanese person who are the three most famous Canadians, he will say Pierre Trudeau, Ben Johnson, and Anne Shirley' (Stoffman 53). Not L.M. Montgomery, mind, but her fictional character. In any discussion of Montgomery's fame, it should be noted that celebrity attaches itself to Anne just as much as to her creator, and abroad, in Japan or in Poland, for instance, Anne arguably eclipses Montgomery as a celebrity figure. Fans will tend to talk about Anne with greater frequency than they talk about Montgomery. In no other instance of Canadian literary celebrity is this the case. It is helpful, I believe, to distinguish between Anne of Green Gables, as a logo, and Montgomery as the celebrity author, not in order to separate them, finally, as celebrity phenomena but to demonstrate the connection, for it proves the intensity and persistence of Montgomery's fame. What she has created has become so famous that it has attained celebrity status in its own right and has circulated through various popular cultural channels while keeping Montgomery's own reflected celebrity alive and thriving, whatever literary academics may say about her canonical status.

On the score of economic rather than cultural capital, Montgomery's success was indisputable during her own lifetime. Clarence Karr estimates that her lifetime earnings, from 23 books, 497 short stories, and 502 poems were 'in excess of $300,000, some of which she invested in blue-chip stocks' (54). This was an incredible amount of money during these years, and it allowed her to educate her two sons, invest for their future, and buy a comfortable home in Toronto when her husband, Ewan Macdonald, always in fragile mental health, retired from his position as a Presbyterian minister. Contemporary accounts made much of the fact that Anne of Green Gables broke the million-sales barrier (Heilbron 183): as Montgomery's longtime literary correspondent Ephraim Weber put it, Anne wore 'the million halo' (ibid. 240). By the time of Montgomery's death, it had gone through sixty-nine printings (Wiggins 36). Her financial success was such that the publisher W.G. Harrap felt the need to add a postscript to Hilda Ridley's 1956 biography of Montgomery, because, in his opinion, that study 'takes little account of the commercial success that attended L.M. Montgomery's work' (141). That is, this early biography paid attention mainly to the cultural capital accumulated by Montgomery, and Harrap wanted to draw some attention to Montgomery as an economic phenomenon. He pointed out that, by 1919, Montgomery's first four titles were out of print, but the deal struck in 1924 between the publishing companies of Page

(Boston), Harrap (London), and Angus and Robertson (Sydney) to publish all the Montgomery titles that they controlled was, according to Harrap, the 'turning point in L.M. Montgomery's climb to fame in Britain and Australia' (142). Even at this relatively early period of Montgomery criticism in the years following her death, there was an explicit conversation going on about how to regard her career: as an impressive achievement of cultural capital or an accumulation of the more monetary kind. In our time, that conversation continues: is Montgomery primarily a valuable academic commodity or a popular cultural phenomenon and lucrative source of tourist dollars?

Before I deal with the infiltration of Montgomery and Anne into present-day popular culture and the tourist economy, I want to pay attention to how Montgomery experienced fame in her lifetime, for, as I have claimed, in her career we have a valuable document of earlier Canadian literary fame. What was fame like for Montgomery, a woman of such quick intelligence and pragmatism that, like Margaret Atwood six decades later, she was well able to diagnose her own condition as a public commodity? Most important, to my mind, Montgomery, who was a sharp-eyed chronicler of community life, gives us an account of how fame sends ripples through one's community of peers. As is true of community life in Avonlea or New Moon, the picture is often not a pretty one. Montgomery carefully noted, in her autobiographical writings, how fame altered her relationships with friends, acquaintances, and family. As she wrote to Ephraim Weber in September 1908, 'If you want to find out just how much *envy* and *petty spite* and *meanness* exists in people, even people who call themselves your friends, just write a successful book or do something they can't do, and you'll find out! ... A certain class of people will take it as a personal insult to themselves, will belittle you and your accomplishment in every way and will go out of their way to make sure that you are informed of their opinions ... I could not begin to tell you all the petty flings of malice and spite of which I have been the target of late, even among some of my own relations' (*Green Gables Letters* 75; emphasis in the original). Another tribulation caused by her fame, which Montgomery would bemoan from time to time, was the tendency of these 'friends' to retell the story of their past relationships with her in their own self-aggrandizing ways. In 1931, over two decades after publishing *Anne of Green Gables*, she records in her journal her frustration at one such retelling of the past, namely John Garvin's claim that he had persuaded Canadian publishers to accept *Anne of Green Gables:* 'To be sure,' Montgomery wearily recounts of an evening with the Authors' Association, 'poor old Garvin came up with his perennial yarn of advising that mythical Toronto firm to "take on" *Green Gables*. I can't remember how many times he has told me that' (*Journals IV;* 107). In another, more painful instance, Montgomery's former teacher, 'Izzie' Robinson told the *Toronto Star* in 1927 that she had been Montgomery's early admirer and mentor, but as Montgomery clearly recalled in her journals, she had actually been very mean to her, and the adult writer had taken her revenge by making her the model for her teacher from hell in *Emily of New Moon*, Miss Brownell (Selected *Journals* 3: 384, 358).

These jealous or self-promoting responses to fame are, of course, well documented, but what aggravates them is precisely that myth of instant success, a part of celebrity rhetoric that underplays the apprenticeship and labour that would, presumably, justify the achievement of success. As with Pauline Johnson, Montgomery's fame narrative obscured the years of patient toil that allowed her to win her world wide audience. As Montgomery confided, once again, to her correspondent Ephraim Weber, 'I've served a long and hard apprenticeship – how hard no one knows but myself. The world only hears of my successes. It *doesn't* hear of all my early buffets and repulses' (*Green Gables Letters* 79–80). In her memoirs, *The Alpine Path*, Montgomery sought to set the record straight. There, she writes feelingly of how 'dreadfully hurt' she felt 'when a story or poem over which I had laboured and agonized came back, with one of those icy rejection slips' (60). And yet, because narratives of success are more welcome than narratives of failure, in everyday life no less than in celebrity discourse, Montgomery kept those failures to herself in her early years: 'I believed in myself and I struggled on alone, in secrecy and silence. I never told my ambitions and efforts and failures to any one' (60). Narratives of failure have little cultural space or recognition unless they are, as in *The Alpine Path*, preludes to a narrative of success. No wonder the past associates of newly minted celebrities often react with jealousy or self-interest; they have consumed the myth of sudden success without its excised twin, the narrative of apprenticeship.

As a compensation for fame, then, literary celebrities must reintroduce the narrative of apprenticeship. This Montgomery does throughout *The Alpine Path*, even, of course, in its title. She opens her account by belittling the very idea that she could have anything so grandiose-sounding as a 'career.' What she has had, instead, has been a 'long, monotonous struggle' (9). The literary celebrity, prey to the glamorization of her literary life narrative, compensates by deglamorizing it. So when Montgomery concludes *The Alpine Path*, she does so by firmly re-emphasizing this idea of a slow, painful struggle, in sweepingly biblical, Bunyanesque language: 'The "Alpine Path" has been climbed, after many years of toil and struggle. It was not an easy ascent' but, rather, a journey 'through bitter suffering and discouragement and darkness, through doubt and disbelief, through valleys of humiliation and over delectable hills where sweet things would lure us from our quest' (95–6). By framing her apprenticeship narrative in religious terms that would have been acceptably humble and labour-oriented to many of her readers, Montgomery finds a socially sanctioned way to appease all of the old jealousies and spite that she has endured over the years as a literary celebrity.

This is, of course, a clever way to advocate for one's own celebrity status, and Montgomery was nothing if not canny and clear-eyed about her fame. In *The Alpine Path*, she accompanies her self-deprecating emphasis on the toil and failures of her apprenticeship period with a corresponding surprise at her success. Still, throughout these passages, there is a sureness of eventual success and recognition that belies her modest surprise. Writing in 1901, long before the international success of *Anne of Green Gables*, Montgomery confided to her journal about the 'landmark' poems that she occasionally writes to mark her progress in artistic achievement: 'A year ago, I could not have written them, but now they come easily and naturally. This encourages me to hope that in the future I may achieve something worth while. I never expect to be famous. I merely want to have a recognized place among good workers in my chosen profession' (Selected Journals, 1: 64). Again, we have the contrast between fame and honest labour that will cause Montgomery so many problems with her friends and family, but it is a distinction to which she, herself, partially subscribes. And, in the final analysis, we have a writer who, under cover of her self-deprecation, is genuinely programmatic about and intent upon making her mark. Though her biographer Mollie Gillen narrated the story of Montgomery's instant success by saying that in 1908, in the weeks following the publication of *Anne of Green Gables*, 'an astounded L.M. Montgomery began to understand that she had produced a best-seller' (71), a less astounded, astute Montgomery knew long before, in some way, that this was the sort of recognition that she had long worked for. As she herself admitted when she came to write the story of her career, 'Down, deep down, under all discouragement and rebuff, I knew I would "arrive" some day' (*Alpine Path* 60).

After 1908, Montgomery was never under any impression that she had not arrived, but, unlike Mazo de la Roche, she did not let her new-found literary celebrity cloud her awareness of her own abilities. She continued to be clear-eyed in her assessment of her literary strengths and weaknesses. When, in the first blush of her publishing success, she cleverly sent out old manuscripts of poems and stories to publishers, she was, in Mollie Gillen's words, 'honest enough to recognize' that a number of them 'sold only because of her new-found fame' (78). She assiduously collected clippings of her many reviews, as is attested by her 'scrapbook of book reviews' in the L.M. Montgomery collection at the University of Guelph, and when she wrote about her reviews in her journals, she tended to give fair hearing to critical treatments of her works, adding to them her own fairly even-handed assessments. On the other hand, when she was challenged in a way that she felt was unfair, as when, in 1930, she was accused in a review of *Magic for Marigold* of using Islanders in her fiction for her own financial benefit, she could state her rights and her achievements as emphatically as any professional agent. As she wrote in reply, 'Yes, "after all," as one of your correspondents so condescendingly remarks ... my books do "travel abroad." My audience is not wholly in Prince Edward Island. And from all over the world thousands of letters come to me annually telling me that my books have filled the writers' wish to see P.E. Island because I have depicted it as such a charming place. Even ... as some of your readers may recall ... so insignificant a person as the Hon. Stanley Baldwin, then Premier of Great Britain, asked the Dominion Government to include Prince Edward Island in his itinerary of 1927 because he had become so interested in it through reading my books' ('L.M. Montgomery's Ideas' 10). This was a woman who knew the extent of her fame. Furthermore, as Elizabeth Epperly has written, Montgomery knew as early as the 1920s that 'she was going to be famous for years to come ... Montgomery intuited that her fame would last well beyond her lifetime' ('Approaching' 74). This is a rare thing for a writer to seem sure of, literary reputations fluctuating as they do. But Montgomery knew it and dealt with the awareness of her likely posthumous fame with the same clarity and pragmatism that she dealt with much else.

One particularly fascinating instance of this pragmatic approach to literary fame is Montgomery's awareness of the likely future value of objects associated with her. She bemoaned the fact that she had not preserved all of her literary manuscripts, for example, and when she finished *Emily of New Moon* in 1922, she 'vowed to keep' it (Epperly, 'Approaching' 74), as 'one day it may have a certain value' (*Selected Journals* 3: 61). Other, less predictable, objects came to have celebrity value for fans of Montgomery's fiction. As early as 1925, Norma Phillips Muir reported in the *Toronto Star Weekly* that some islanders, welcoming visitors to their homes, offer them 'the chair L.M. Montgomery sat in, when she was here' (Heilbron 230). Montgomery herself realized, as the years went on, that domestic objects associated with her would accrue this sort of touristic value. In her journals she recounts coming across some pieces of lacework in 1930 that she had made as a young woman for her hope chest, and she ruefully notes that 'they may have a value someday because "L.M. Montgomery" made them' (*Selected Journals* 4: 49–50). Montgomery was fully borne out in her calculations of the role of her domestic objects in the extensive tourist industry associated with her literary reputation. The literary birthplace of Montgomery in New London, PEI, has her wedding dress, veil, and shoes on display, and the Anne of Green Gables Museum at Silver Bush boasts 'handicrafts once owned by the author' (Colombo 54). In 1997 the L.M. Montgomery Institute, housed at the University of Prince Edward Island, received, from a local donor, a complete set of Montgomery's novels, many of them first editions and autographed by the author and 'a bedspread hand-knit by the author' ('News from the L.M. Montgomery Institute'). Montgomery's presentiments as to the likely value – in cultural capital terms, here – of her domestic handiwork were all too accurate. Bedspreads and lacework share cultural space with the author's writings, as objects of celebrity devotion.

If Montgomery's handiwork qualifies as an object of consumption today, her clothes and hair arrangements were no less objects of remark in her own day. This was particularly apparent when Montgomery made her first major foray into promotional touring, to Boston in November 1910. She was besieged by journalists and admirers, and in the press coverage, her appearance seemed to attract particular comment. As one reporter from the *Boston Republic* noted on 19 November, 'Miss Montgomery is short and slight, indeed of a form almost childishly small, though graceful and symmetrical. She has an oval face, with delicate aquiline features, bluish-grey eyes and an abundance of dark brown hair. Her pretty pink evening gown somewhat accentuated her frail and youthful aspect' ('Red Scrapbook #1'). The attention to the physiognomy of the famous writer is familiar, in the case of celebrated male and female authors alike, but the additional attention to dresses and other accoutrements was Montgomery's due as a woman writer at the time. Looking through the scrapbook she kept during the time of her Boston tour, which contains many such press notices, this careful attention to the details of Montgomery's dress is everywhere, obsessively so at times. The newspapers ran fashion-image photographs of Montgomery, clad in a fur-trimmed coat and fashionably veiled hat ('Red Scrapbook #1'). Of course, such attention was not limited to her much-publicized trip to Boston. In a later scrapbook item, detailing Montgomery's speech to the Canadian Business Women's club in Hamilton, the *Hamilton Spectator* journalist is at great pains to describe the now older author's hair style: 'thick hair, slightly graying, which she wore waved and coiled becomingly about her well-shaped head' ('Red Scrapbook #2'). This is the sort of scrutiny of women writers' physical appearances that a later novelist, Margaret Atwood, would roundly satirize in *Lady Oracle*, in, for instance, the media's fascination with novelist Joan Foster's crowning glory, her curly red tresses.

As this pervasive scrutiny of the personal suggests, Montgomery, like Mazo de la Roche, knew what it was to negotiate the public and the private in the face of wide publicity. Unlike de la Roche, however, Montgomery did not particularly pursue the limelight, under cover of wishing not to. She was irked by the sort of newspaper scrutiny that delved into her personal life; as she wrote to her friend G.B. MacMillan in 1909, 'I don't care what they do about my book – *it* is public property – but I wish they would leave my *ego* alone' (*My Dear Mr. M* 44). Montgomery wished to rely upon a simple, pragmatic division between the public product, the writing, and the private entity, the writer, but the celebrity culture that was taking shape in North America during the years she experienced her success militated against any such easy division. As one newspaper snippet from her scrapbook of book reviews, dating sometime during her residence at Leaskdale, Ontario, reveals, the distinction between private and public was porous to the point of becoming a comic illusion. After quoting Montgomery's reasons for not entering a Prince Edward Island writing competition, the journalist concludes, 'Her words, above quoted, although not intended for publication, are an inspiration also and we commend them to our readers' ('Scrapbook of Book Reviews'). So much for an 'off-the-record' comment. On one occasion, Montgomery was so irked by a particularly fanciful interview with her that she clipped it, pasted it into her scrapbook, and wrote under the byline, 'This "interview" is fiction from beginning to end' ('Scrapbook of Book Reviews'). Like Mazo de la Roche, Montgomery used private textual space like a scrapbook to intervene in public representations of herself that she found distasteful, but such intervention was, of course, limited in its effects.

Although critics have made much of Montgomery's ability to carry on a private life, as Mrs Ewan Macdonald, the wife of a minister, it is clear that this supposed protection of privacy was, actually, a complicated balancing act that often left the private under increasing pressure. As Alexandra Heilbron recounts, 'when young fans phoned Maud at her home, she graciously spoke with them – she was never rude or impatient about having been disturbed at home. She granted interviews to anyone who requested one, even schoolgirls writing for their school paper ... She was generous with her time, even though she often had so little to spare' (159). In her book, Heilbron reprints several such remembrances of Montgomery, from some of those young girls whom Montgomery helped or church members whose small congregations Montgomery spoke to. It sounds like the perfect marriage of a public and a private life, and yet readers of Montgomery's journals know how frantically exhausted Montgomery often was, trying to keep up with the day-to-day demands of being a minister's wife, the spouse of an increasingly ill man, and the mother of two boys, while taking on enormous numbers of speaking engagements and the like. Indeed, the tension between public and private probably shortened Montgomery's life.

Another drain on Montgomery's already pressured life was the time she needed to give over to answer fan mail. Like Mazo de la Roche, Montgomery received a large volume of such mail, and, again like de la Roche, she answered it herself (Heilbron

159), a fact that is difficult to absorb, given all the other demands on Montgomery's time. In Montgomery's case, she received a fair amount of this mail from children: she loved to tell about children writing to Anne Shirley at Green Gables. (A tribute to the post office of the day as well as to Montgomery's fame: the PEI post office knew exactly where to deliver those letters.) As Hilda Ridley enumerated, Montgomery received mail from 'soldiers in India, missionaries in China, traders in Africa, monks in far-away monasteries, and from trappers in the Canadian North' (92). Was any place on earth free of the red-haired orphan and her creator? Apparently not. As Montgomery once wearily reflected, 'I think every red-haired girl in the world must have written to me' (Heilbron 188).

However weary she was – and readers of her journals now know how very often she felt worn out and exhausted – Montgomery worked hard to fulfill all of the roles that she felt she was given in her life. As a result, what we have in stronger measure than in any of the other earlier literary celebrities I examine, is the effect of celebrity on negotiations of women's roles, as traditionally defined. In her collection of oral remembrances of Montgomery, *Remembering Lucy Maud Montgomery*, Alexandra Heilbron's section divisions are suggestive of this crowding of roles: 'Maud, Beloved Aunt and Grandmother'; 'Mrs. Macdonald as an Employer'; 'Maud as Neighbour and Friend'; 'Mrs. Macdonald, Our Sunday School Teacher'; and, finally, as a kind of crowning, but inclusive role, 'L.M. Montgomery, Famous Author.' Montgomery's fame had to make room for all of the other roles Heilbron lists and many more besides. Even the alternate namings of Montgomery as 'Maud' and 'Mrs. Macdonald' in Heilbron's list signal the tensions inherent in such an act of role inclusion. Montgomery herself loved to tell a humorous story that reveals how difficult people could find it to regard her as the possessor of multiple roles. When she returned, as she often did, from Ontario to Prince Edward Island for a visit on one occasion, the local newspaper announced that 'Miss. L.M. Montgomery' had arrived for a visit with her young son. Of course, in the social parlance of the time, this would have suggested that Montgomery was an unmarried mother, something still thought quite shocking in Montgomery's circles, so Montgomery would tell the story as a comic one, protesting that she was not quite the modern woman the newspaper evidently thought her. And yet, the confusion that reigned at this time when a 'Miss L.M. Montgomery' who writes books had to be reconciled with a Mrs Macdonald who raises children has its less than comic aspect ('Red Scrapbook #2').

As the canny celebrity that she was, Montgomery knew that there were times in her life when it would be advantageous for her to play 'Miss L.M. Montgomery' rather than 'Mrs. Macdonald,' but she almost never did. One of the most poignant occasions of this temptation was her visit, in February 1930 with her husband, Ewan, to their son Chester's school, Knox College, in Toronto, to deal with reports of the boy's failing academic work. The secretary and chair of the college were both condescending to her and to Ewan and, to make matters even more humiliating, the interview concluded with Montgomery breaking her pearl necklace and having to ignominiously scramble about to retrieve the pearls that had cascaded across the floor. Montgomery later bitterly recorded in her journal, 'I have never felt so *insignificant.*' As though instantly reminded of the realm in which she was, by contrast, accorded great personal significance, Montgomery mused, 'I wonder if those men had known I was "L.M. Montgomery" if they would not have been a little more considerate. I have often seen it work out so. But I took good care they should not know. I shall always remember just how they behaved to plain, obscure, countrified Mrs. Ewan Macdonald' (*Selected Journals* 4: 105). The celebrity card was one that Montgomery had readily at hand but rarely played, the better, perhaps, to observe the manifold workings of power around her as a woman.

The role conflicts occasioned by Montgomery's celebrity were not made any easier by her knowledge that, in Mary Rubio's words, her husband 'manifested a deep underlying hostility to her success as a writer' (8). The germs of that hostility appear in some of the newspaper clippings of Montgomery's wedding to

Ewan Macdonald. One, rather ominously, is headlined, 'Famous
Authoress Weds a Minister' and subtitled 'Miss Montgomery of
Charlottetown, Who Wrote "Ann [sic] of Green Gables" Married
to Ontario Pastor' ('Red Scrapbook #1'). Clearly, Macdonald
seemed doomed to anonymity in this domestic alliance, a situation few men of the time would have found the resources to deal
with. Macdonald's growing resentment of her fame must have
been very hard for her to bear, particularly when Montgomery
also had to face the press's constant questions about how she
managed to combine her many roles. In her scrapbooks she collected many instances of interviews in which journalists mar-
velled over her multiple roles, clearly suggesting that to
combine authorship and the life of a minister's wife was unconventional and odd. As C.L. Cowan exclaimed in the *Toronto Star
Weekly* in 1928, 'this was a new experience to meet a literary
celebrity who was also a parson's wife' (Heilbron 231). Several
journalists were fixated upon Montgomery's role as a mother of
two young children and hastened to assure their readers that
her first priority lay with their care (and not, by implication, with
her writing): 'One could see that Mrs. E. Macdonald – or L.M.
Montgomery as the world prefers to call her – is a proud
mother' (Heilbron 234). Fittingly, in demonstrating the primacy
of the maternal role, the journalist also asserted the primacy of
Montgomery's married name. Ethel Chapman, in her profile of
'The Author of Anne' in *Maclean's*, October 1919, makes Montgomery's maternal priorities clear, but rather anxiously: 'The
author of Anne does not devote herself entirely to the making of
books ... She is a mother who mothers her children personally;
they have always been considered before her books' (Heilbron
199). As a much later novelist, Carol Shields, once wrote of her
fictional author and mother figure, Reta Winters in *Unless*,
'"How did you find the time?" people used to chorus, and in that
query I often registered a hit of blame: was I neglecting my darling sprogs for my writing career?' (4). Sadly, it seems, not much
may have changed in regard to women, literary success, and
domestic roles since Montgomery's time: mothers' writing is still
thought, in some quarters, to place the sprogs at risk.

Again, as with literary celebrities such as Pauline Johnson, it is easy to chronicle the ways in which celebrity confined and restricted the literary star, and in the case of Montgomery and her role conflict, her frequent exhaustion, and her painful awareness of the jealousies of others, it is particularly easy to do. But for Montgomery, too, fame brought expanded possibilities to make contact with major political figures and to intervene in some of the most pressing social questions of the day. Her celebrity was confirmed by the notice that significant political figures took of her writing. In September 1910, Governor General Earl Grey telegrammed Montgomery to request a visit when he next came to Charlottetown, and British Prime Minister Stanley Baldwin made a particular point of stopping in Prince Edward Island to meet her. As he was to remark in the 1930s, 'I've read every Montgomery book I could get my hands on two and three times over' (Gillen 157). Mary Rubio argues that because the political world of the first quarter of the twentieth century was so 'disordered,' political leaders might well respond favourably to a fictional world in which a 'pattern of order, disruption, renegotiation, and a re-established (if a slightly modified) order, provided solace' (6). Also, the bucolic scenes that Montgomery's books offered must have seemed similarly soothing in a time of rapid industrialization, militarization and global war.

Montgomery did more than simply meet major political figures. Her opinion was sought, published, and listened to, on questions like Canadian publishing policy, women's suffrage, and the world wars. As Irene Gammel and Elizabeth Epperly maintain, 'Montgomery's opinion made an impact in the daily media, and in 1923 the *Toronto Star* listed her as one of the twelve greatest women in Canada' ('Introduction' 3). For example, the periodical *Everywoman's World* asked Montgomery to ponder two questions: What did she hope to see as the outcome of the First World War, and what did she hope to see by way of outcome for women in particular? Montgomery struck a much less conservative note than usual, noting that 'the women who bear and train the nation's sons should have some voice in the

political issues that may send those sons to die on battlefields'
('Red Scrapbook #1'). On one occasion, Montgomery shared
the podium with British suffrage leader Emmeline Pankhurst,
but her theme was not women's enfranchisement on this occasion; instead, she spoke of the need for the Canadian reading
public to buy more Canadian books. Montgomery's advice, that
one book out of three bought by a household should be Canadian, received extensive media coverage ('Red Scrapbook #2').
When the figure of the flapper became the fashion in the twenties, again Montgomery was asked to comment. Again, she
responded in a less conservative fashion than one might expect,
pointing out that 'every generation ... thinks that the present
one is bound to perdition, while the scandalized ones were
probably the despair of their own parents' ('Red Scrapbook
#2'). When one reads through these lively interviews on matters
of public policy, cultural trends, and politics, the overwhelming
impression is of a woman who is entirely comfortable with her
own ability to speak on a national stage about a wide range of
subjects. For all of the private tension and public scepticism
about her role as a public Canadian, Montgomery performed it
with a sense of utter entitlement.

For all that she was in the public eye for so many years, a ster-
ling example of international literary fame and a source of commentary on a number of social issues, Montgomery suffered the
fate of most popular writers of the early twentieth century: academic devaluation. Elizabeth Epperly traces the critical dismissal of Montgomery in the middle years of the century and
cites the main reasons for it: Montgomery was popular, Canadian, female, and a children's writer ('L.M. Montgomery' 179).
As in Carole Gerson's analysis of Pauline Johnson, Mary Rubio
blames mainly the advent of literary modernism, and its penchant for segregating high and low culture, for Montgomery's
decline (4–5). As with Mazo de la Roche, however, no matter
how Montgomery's academic reputation has fared (and
recently it has begun, unlike de la Roche's, to make a significant
comeback), her fan base has continued strong, attracting, in
Epperly's words, 'perennial popularity in North America, Brit-

ain, and Australia' (where her books were kept in print through a publishers' agreement) and 'phenomenal popularity in Japan and Poland' ('L.M. Montgomery" 184). Still, the tension between popularity and critical esteem continues to plague Montgomery's reputation. Margaret Atwood opens her short reflection piece, 'Revisiting Anne,' by admitting that '*Anne of Green Gables* is one of those books you feel almost guilty liking, because so many other people seem to like it as well. If it's that popular, you feel, it can't possibly be good, or good for you' (222). This seems classic Bourdieusian sociology; the quality of the aesthetic product is proved, ironically, by its lack of consumers, but this prejudice predates the major movement of literary modernism in Canada. In 1910, when Montgomery published *Kilmeny of the Orchard*, just two years after her runaway success with *Anne of Green Gables*, one critic complained that the new novel showed signs of 'the insidious influence of popularity and success' (Hill 23). Montgomery loved to tell this story, because she had composed *Kilmeny of the Orchard* long before *Anne*. So much for 'insidious influence.' But wherever there is popularity, a critic will be sure to blame its workings.

As with Mazo de la Roche, the sequel plays a role in this damning of Montgomery's work for its insidious popularity. But whereas de la Roche became increasingly attached to her sequels, even as her publishers and reviewers became steadily disaffected, Montgomery seems genuinely to have wished to quit them. As Holly Pike argues, Montgomery 'was committed to the Anne material for financial reasons' (56). There is plenty of evidence in the journals that Montgomery did, indeed, resent the financial inducements that led to her placate her publishers by offering them yet more and more of Anne. She knew she must 'cater to [the public] for awhile yet' (*Selected Journals* 3: 157). Montgomery did manage to write much else that had nothing to do with Anne, but however well those works sold, they could not touch *Anne* and her sequels in point of popularity. In terms of critical appraisal, it has long been a commonplace to dismiss the sequels, implicitly seeing them as the product of marketing forces rather than artistic inspiration. Of course, assuming that a first novel is purer, belonging more to the realm of aesthetics than commerce, denies its role in a market economy. And although Montgomery, as a very young woman, may have been surprised at her first payment for a published poem (Gillen 33), she very soon became a professional writer who was seriously concerned with the business side of her career. As Carole Gerson has noted, Montgomery was a 'canny businesswoman' ('Dragged' 146).

In fact, Gerson, like Ruth Panofsky writing about Mazo de la Roche, is notable for defending Montgomery's use of the sequel, resisting the common critical tendency to see it as a sign of artistic weakness and (corresponding) worldly greed. Reintroducing the hushed topic of economics in literary analysis of Canadian works, she argues that Montgomery's second book, *Anne of Avonlea*, was 'generated not by the clamour of enchanted readers, but by the current practices of market publishing' ('Dragged' 149), though the two are, admittedly, often closely intertwined. Publishers anticipate, or perhaps anticipate *creating*, the clamour of enchanted readers – and buyers. On the related question of the aesthetic value of sequels, Gerson also questions the commonplace in earlier Montgomery criticism that the sequels were disappointing. Again introducing the repressed topic of the economic, she points to the profits realized by them and by other spin-off cultural artifacts like television series, souvenirs, and musicals: 'Disappointing for whom?' she asks (ibid. 145). There must have been a considerable fan base that did not experience total disappointment. This is another instance of the small-production aesthetic claiming all territory as its own, and so concealing other ways in which texts may be consumed, for other reasons.

If one adopts this approach to Montgomery's fame in general, tourism clearly becomes another site of contestation for notions of high and popular culture. Literary tourism, viewed from the perspective of small-production culture, is an open challenge to the very notion of high culture, because by definition, it involves the mass consumption of an author and works that are thought best if fully accessible only by the few. Besides, as Calvin Trillin has written, authors often do not seem to make attractive candidates for tourism because it can be difficult to publicize an activity that is, in many respects, intensely private: 'Normally, I think, exploiting an author as a tourist attraction presents a problem that also crops up in writing an author's biography: What's to see? The labor that makes a world-famous novelist worth writing about was almost certainly done while he was sitting all by himself in a quiet room' (217). Yet, Trillin goes on to say, Montgomery was so intensely associated with certain landscapes (as were, of course, other touristically marketable literary celebrities such as Hemingway and Wordsworth), that this problem is largely overcome. The development of Cavendish and other Montgomery points of interest on Prince Edward Island proves Trillin right. All of these manifestations of her celebrity, and of the celebrity of her logo or trademark, Anne, mark a contest over the cultural ownership of Montgomery: elite or mass culture?

More than any other literary celebrity in Canadian history, L.M. Montgomery has become the foundation of a major international tourist industry. Unlike the Leacock-related tourist developments in Orillia, with their sluggish beginnings and bumpy history, the Montgomery industry was thriving in the author's own lifetime. This is another respect in which Montgomery and her autobiographical writings, most notably her journals, have been rich archives of early Canadian literary celebrity: they show her in the process of assessing and responding to her own status as a tourist attraction. It did not take long after the success of *Anne of Green Gables* for visitors to Prince Edward Island to try to find their way to Montgomery's door. By 1929, a little over two decades later, there existed the trappings of a modern tourist industry in Cavendish – so much so that Montgomery, home for a visit, bitterly vented her frustration at the commodification of her past. Taking a walk along her beloved shore, she 'lingered there for an hour – alone – all alone with my old love. There were no intrusive crowds that night – no raucous cars – no hot dogs!' (*Selected Journals* 4: 12). By that year plans were also afoot to turn into historical sites a number of buildings made significant by their association with the famous author. These plans, too, Montgomery assessed with biting sarcasm, to the point that she was glad to contemplate what had been one of her most painful memories – the destruction of her childhood home: 'Uncle John is *very* sorry he tore the old house down. Very sorry indeed. And why! Because it has lately dawned on him that he could have made money over it. Crowds of people go there to see it – or the place where it was ... *Frank*, too, has been heard to lament the destruction. If the house were in existence his wife would come over and run a tea-room there in the summer for tourists! ... I am glad the old house has gone. It can never be degraded to the uses of a tea-room' (*Journals* 4: 11). Hot dogs and tea rooms: these were, in Montgomery's eyes, horrors of commodification, displaced objects of consumption for what was really up for sale: Montgomery herself.

Still, Montgomery's response to the development of Cavendish and other nearby sites altered as the years went on. By 1936, according to Mollie Gillen, Montgomery still felt it was 'sacrilege to make her private haunts public tourist spots, but she also realized that this would prevent the land being broken up into individual holdings – trees would be cut down and lanes destroyed' (181). In effect, what Montgomery was pragmatic enough to help prevent was what befell the Leacock property at Old Brewery Bay, with the sectioning off of private lands, a process that very nearly destroyed the possibility of a monument to Leacock. As a result, Green Gables, the elaborately constructed tourist fiction, succeeded beyond anyone's wildest dreams and has become one of the main means by which Montgomery's celebrity is reconfirmed and kept alive. In fact, according to Diane Tye, Montgomery as a celebrity has taken over the cultural space that was the community of Cavendish: 'Tourism's appropriation of community space is almost complete, as the affiliation with Montgomery of usually community-owned spaces like the post office (identified as Green Gables) and the cemetery (bearing the name "Lucy Maud Montgomery's Resting Place") demonstrate' (126). Tye's second example is a particularly eerie instance of a celebrity deriving continued life from a community; the iron bower that forms the entranceway to the cemetery reads, actually, 'Resting Place of L.M. Montgomery' and then, underneath that, in much smaller letters, 'Cavendish.' One wonders how families of others who rest there feel about Montgomery becoming the synecdoche for all of the Cavendish ancestors. It seems a strange kind of celebrity vampirism visited upon a community-host.

In the case of Montgomery, more so than any other literary celebrity I study here, the sites associated with her life and career are consistently set up as objects of reverence. 'The most famous literary shrine in the country,' John Robert Colombo dubs the Green Gables historical site in Cavendish (50). Part of the reason for the religious awe is the crucial decision to restore the house, not simply as a period piece, but as a dramatic re-enactment of the setting of Montgomery's famous first novel. As a result, the tourist visiting the Green Gables house at Cavendish enters a space that is fictive, and anyone who has entered that space can attest to the way in which fellow tourists consume the setting as though the fiction and the present scene before them were interchangeable: 'That's Anne's room' or 'Here's where Marilla would cook the meals' are the sorts of comments frequently heard in the house. Souvenirs sold on site encourage this fictive reading of the attraction; postcards of the rooms, for instance, refer to the room in the novel that is being represented: 'Anne's room'; 'Marilla's room.' All of this lends the touristic scene a touch of ritual, of sacred re-enactment. The same is true of the Anne of Green Gables Museum at Silver Bush, Park Corner, PEI, where, every year, there is a ritual re-enactment of Montgomery's marriage, in the room where the event actually took place. Tourists may book a special wedding package that involves being married there too and then being escorted for a horse and buggy ride along the fictional Lake of Shining Waters. (Given the desperately unhappy fate of Montgomery's marriage, it seems mysterious that this portion of the literary star's life should attract such devoted repetition.) Events both fictional and historical get blithely mixed together in this act of reverential re-enactment. The title of Nancy Rootland's lovely coffee-table volume says it best, if a touch comically: *The Sacred Sites of L.M. Montgomery.*

Far from the sacred sites of Montgomery's PEI fame, the Anne of Green Gables industry thrives abroad, and in the last few years critics have been investigating the possible causes for Montgomery's phenomenal celebrity in countries like Japan and Poland. In terms of popularity abroad, no Canadian writer before or since Montgomery can rival her. She has become the textbook case of the Canadian literary celebrity who, like Hemingway in the United States, operates internationally as a marketing logo long after her death. The infiltration of the Anne saga abroad started early, like many other aspects of Montgomery's celebrity. In 1912, *Anne of Green Gables* was translated into Swedish, Dutch, and Polish, and proceeded to attain strongholds in all three cultures. (For example, Swedish children's writer Astrid Lindgren, author of the Pippi Longstocking novels, has claimed that she was indebted to Montgomery for aspects of her red-headed, irrepressible heroine [Wiggins 37].) After 1912, Poland became and remains one of the strongholds of Anne fandom. In the aftermath of the Second World War, the government saw Montgomery's books as 'potentially dangerous' and duly tried to ban them (Rubio 8), causing a tremendous backlash, as such government edicts in Poland often tended to do. In the case of Japan, the other major hot-spot of Montgomery popularity, the translation appeared after the Second World War, in 1952, just as Japan was experiencing the large-scale infiltration of so many other North American cultural products. And as it did with so many of those American products, Japan embraced *Akage no An* (Red-haired Anne) with a fervour that took many Canadians by surprise three decades later, when a Tokyo publisher started the massive Japanese Anne of Green Gables tourism industry by organizing a tour to Prince Edward Island for enthusiastic fans (Akamatsu 210). In fact, it was this massive market for all things Anne that first created trouble between Montgomery's heirs and Kevin Sullivan, producer of the immensely popular *Anne* series of television specials and spinoff *Road to Avonlea* series. Once the immensity of the Japanese market began to be appreciated in the 1980s, Sullivan applied for trademarks there without informing the family that he had done so (Ross, 'Battle of Avonlea'). As Judy Stoffman has rightly observed of the Japanese Anne figure, An, she 'is more than a literary figure [in Japan]. She is a commercial icon' (55), and the literary heirs of L.M. Montgomery did not appreciate being left out of the transaction.

From the point of view of celebrity culture, what is important about this surge in Montgomery's fame abroad, especially in countries like Japan and Poland, is the way in which it has accelerated the introduction of Montgomery and her works into other facets of popular culture, in those countries and in Canada. Judy Stoffman and Yoshiko Akamatsu produce a number of examples, many of them quite humorous: Japanese Anne fan clubs with names like Lupins and Tribe of Anne, an Okayama City nursing school called 'The School of Green Gables' (Akamatsu 205, 206) that presumably wishes to instill Anne's love of learning and care for others (such as the aging Marilla), a scale model of Green Gables fashioned in sugar (Stoffman 57–8), Pokemon-style Anne comic books and much else besides. At home, critics such as Jeanette Lynes have started to analyse the import of Anne commodities that are sold nationwide but, most intensively, in Cavendish and Charlottetown: dolls, CD-Roms, calendars, mouse pads ... Lynes surveys the various wares for sale at the Anne of Green Gables store in Charlottetown, linking it with the more general trend in merchandising towards the country store model. This is the popular contemporary phenomenon of stores like 'the General Store' or 'the Whippletree' in urban and suburban malls, selling country-style products and, in effect, selling a simulacrum of rural values to urban customers. My own collection of Anne merchandising includes several flyers from the Cavendish area advertising tourist industry real estate: Anne Shirley Motel and Cottages, Shining Waters Resort and (my own favourite for reasons of utter incommensurability) Anne's Whispering Pines RV Park. Avonlea has truly, in Lynes's phrase, become 'a floating signifier' (10) in a mass-merchandising industry. Until very recently, however, this mass com-modification of Montgomery was not analysed by academics; the first route that they took in reintroducing Montgomery to a small-production cultural audience was, instead, to argue for her inclusion in the canon of significant Canadian writers. Now, after some years, Montgomery's overwhelming presence in pop-ular culture is finally receiving some sustained attention and analysis.

Clearly, Montgomery has been the most successful, most internationally recognized example of a Canadian literary celebrity, and her career and continuing celebrity and market-ability highlight the complex interactions of cultural and liter-ary capital during her lifetime and today. Still, all of the earlier celebrities I have examined here have made their travels through the realms of high and popular culture and have lived with their apparent accommodations and contradictions. Though they did not self-consciously explore tropes of celebrity in their work, for the most part this was no golden age of inno-cence, no edenic pre-celebrity garden, where books were pub-lished on merit alone and authors stayed in the dreamt-of Joycean background, 'invisible, refined out of existence, indif-ferent, paring' their 'fingernails.' Pauline Johnson, Stephen Leacock, Mazo de la Roche, and Lucy Maud Montgomery were no wide-eyed innocents untouched by the forces, tensions, and pleasures of celebrity. Instead, they were in the very thick of developing and competing ideas about who authors are, as eco-nomic and cultural bodies, during the opening decades of the twentieth century. As such, they set the stage for the challenges faced by later Canadian literary stars such as Margaret Atwood, Michael Ondaatje, and Carol Shields: they do not signal an age when those challenges did not exist.

3 Margaret Atwood's 'Uneasy Eminence': Negotiating with the Famous

I've been described as the Barbra Streisand of Can Lit ... But I think of myself more as the Mary Pickford, spreading joy.

Margaret Atwood

Back in 1973, quite early in her celebrated career, Margaret Atwood offered the above tongue-in-cheek description of her public persona. Jocular though it was, it offers several points of entry into the topic of her celebrity status. Most superficially, it shows, though its awareness of the resemblance a younger Atwood bore to the then-popular American diva, Barbra Streisand, a corresponding awareness of the role that physical appearance plays in her celebrity; as numerous commentators have observed, Atwood's features have become a trademark of sorts. And it also signals the uneasy relation between Atwood's North American and nationally specific Canadian celebrity; her chosen celebrity persona, Mary Pickford, was a Canadian-born star of the early screen who earned the title of America's Sweetheart south of the border. As many observers of Atwood's literary celebrity will attest, Atwood, too, has been appropriated as an American writer (Owens). As Caroline Rosenthal has discovered from surveying American teachers of Atwood, 'Many ... responded that they have taught a variety of Atwood's works, including her essays, but did not identify her as a Canadian' (46). But more broadly, Atwood's off-the-cuff comment is remarkable simply for its self-consciousness; even in 1973, just one year after Atwood came to national attention with the publication of *Survival*, she is offering a meta-commentary on her own celebrity.

This self-conscious awareness of the terms of her own celebrity is what sets Atwood apart from the other two contemporary Canadian literary stars I examine in this study. Among Canadian writers from the past five decades, Atwood offers the sort of clear-eyed analysis of the celebrity experience that L.M. Montgomery before her came closest to formulating. If Atwood is often thought of as the Canadian literary celebrity par excellence, she is no less a shrewd analyst of its terms and tendencies. On several occasions, she has even parodied her own star text – the conglomeration of her celebrity meanings – producing a list of quintessentially Atwoodian public personas: 'Witch, man-hater, man-freezing Medusa, man-devouring monster. The Ice Goddess. The Snow Queen' (Atwood, 'If You Can't' 20); 'Margaret the Monster and Margaret the Magician and Margaret the Mother' (MacGregor 66). As Susanne Becker perceptively notes, such persona parodies serve both to describe but also to contain media representations (32); they are, in a sense, critical pre-emptive strikes of a particularly.clever sort.

Of course, Atwood's great measure of self-consciousness is partly a reflection of the extensive nature of the celebrity system that represents her to a broad audience. Graham Huggan, in his book *The Postcolonial Exotic*, devotes a full chapter to what he calls 'Margaret Atwood, Inc.' or the 'Atwood industry.' And Susanne Becker, a German scholar whose geographical placement evinces Atwood's global appeal, has offered an academic reading of 'Celebrity, or a Disneyland of the Soul: Margaret Atwood and the Media.' So Atwood's own heightened self-consciousness of her stardom mirrors the meta-criticism of her celebrity that is beginning, in recent years, to enter the scholarship devoted to her. Some of this criticism, like Becker's, reveals how Atwood cannily uses the media; other critics, like Huggan, explore the reasons for Atwood's remarkable success in world literary markets. He points to several factors: first and foremost her hard work and productivity; her ability to speak eloquently on a wide range of subjects both literary and political; her manifold roles as writer, feminist, environmentalist, nationalist; what he calls 'the soundbite quality of her public utterances' and 'epigrammatic witticisms' that render her media-friendly; and her launching of subversive attacks on social mores from the protected position of the middle class (214–17). As important as all of this work on the canonization of Atwood is, my own project is not to establish and explain Atwood's celebrity. Instead of asking *why* Atwood is a star, I will direct attention to *how* both she and her works are read in terms of celebrity and, in turn, how she actively intervenes in those readings. I contend that her intervention is both powerfully shrewd and subtly uneasy in a number of ways.

Beginning with superficialities, I first examine the pervasive attention that has been focused on Atwood as a visual spectacle. This obsession with her appearance eclipses the attention paid to any previous Canadian writer's personal presentation, bar none. One might point to the Stephen Leacock figure of the rumpled philosopher, or to the equally rumpled physical persona of Mordecai Richler, both of which inspired a certain amount of nostalgic warmth among Canadian audiences, but neither Leacock nor Richler, nor any other figure in our literary history I can think of, has had such unremitting attention directed to his or her physical appearance. By the 1980s, as Susanne Becker notes, Atwood became a frequent cover-girl for a number of Canadian national magazines. By that time, physical descriptions of Atwood had become such ready coinage that journalists who sought to profile her were complaining that they were quickly running out of untried adjectives. Journalist Judith Timson, writing for the popular women's magazine *Chatelaine*, explained: 'Writing about Margaret Atwood has become no easy task – all the descriptions for her hair have already been used up: that "familiar wreath of disorganized hair," that "nimbus of crinkled curls," that "kinky flyaway hairstyle that is her trademark"' (60, 64). Timson was directly quoting previous journalists' descriptions; the suggestive 'nimbus of crinkled curls,' for instance, appeared in a profile by Adele Freedman in the *Globe and Mail* just a year before Timson sought out her adjectives in 1981. By the end of the nineties, the visual branding of Atwood had become a continental phenomenon; in 1997, the large American bookstore chain Barnes and Noble displayed the curly-locked Atwood on its plastic bags (flipside to Charles Dickens, that veritable touchstone of literary celebrity) (Ayre D14).

As far as conceptualizations of celebrity are concerned, this branding of Atwood would suggest, at first glance, an open-and-closed case of celebrity manufacture, a relatively straightforward case of the visual commodification of a passive, objectified star. But rather than take up this theory of celebrity manufacture, I would direct attention, instead, to the way in which Atwood intervenes in even this seemingly inescapable manipulation of her celebrity image. There are several ways in which she does this. For one thing, she has proved herself adept at ridiculing such representations; she once noted that an enterprising critic had actually done a study of her book-jacket photographs and had decided that there were 'not enough smiles, in her opinion. Girls, like the peasants in eighteenth-century genre paintings, are supposed to smile a lot' (Atwood, 'If You Can't' 20). At one stroke, Atwood both shows a keen awareness of the gaze of others and identifies its gendered investments.

Another counter-commodifying strategy at Atwood's disposal is self-deprecating humour. As she commented to Adele Freedman, 'Now people say I'm beautiful; before I was famous, they just said "Can't you do something with your hair?"' (E1). Atwood takes the primary visual signifier in her public image and both acknowledges and deflates its celebrity commodification. Fittingly, Atwood also turns to a visual medium – comic strips – to accomplish a similar double-edged self-parody. For years she has drawn comics, often devoted to witty reflections on her own career or to current political events. On her Web site (www.owtoad.com), at this time of writing, she has four comics depicting the pitfalls of going on book tours: being

interviewed by bumptious, rude interviewers and by interviewers who have not read the book, and facing negative reviews.
And in all of these comics she has depicted herself as a short
woman with squiggles for hair, dressed in black boots and dress,
topped by a dramatic arty hat that bears an unsettling resemblance to a witch's cap. Many of the stock descriptions of her
physical appearance are on full display here, and, by co-opting
and reproducing them, Atwood intervenes and recaptures the
power of the gaze. As Nathalie Cooke writes of some of the earlier comics, in which Atwood parodically represents herself as
'Survivalwoman,' 'Atwood presents Atwood as short and soft-
spoken, buried under a mass of curls ... These cartoon or stick
figures are self-deprecating and funny, proof that Atwood takes
her work seriously but does not take herself too seriously' (22).
And while that is certainly true, they are both deflation and
acknowledgment of her celebrity status. Atwood refashions herself, but this act not only disrupts a commodifying gaze; it also
confirms it.

Some of Atwood's recent public addresses reveal a similar
strategy of revisualization. When she spoke before a group of
scholars and readers at the University of Ottawa in 2004, for
instance, her presentation took the form of a slide show of personal photographs, another version of the autobiographical
comic strip. These photos, arranged in chronological order like
the selected photos that she has included on her Web site, also
drew upon Atwood's quick, self-deprecating wit ('This is me
dressed up as a triangle,' ran one terse commentary). But they
also included visualizations of parts of her life that Atwood has
resolutely told people are none of their business; she included,
for instance, a rather grainy photograph of her first marriage.
And her photographs of her daughter, Jess, were offered with
warmth and affectionate humour. Her final photograph showed
her shaking the hand of the Queen of England. Her dry reflection: 'Only one of these women is the Queen of England.' Here
is another instance of a penetrating awareness of the celebrity
representations of Atwood that have circulated in the Canadian
literary world: Margaret the Queen Bee. So, on one hand, we

have the workings of a self-deflating, hole-poking parody of Atwood as an all-powerful icon. But we also have a reinforcement of that very iconicity.

Personas are often an attempt to pre-empt critical inquiry or plain prurience; as some critics of Hemingway's larger-than-life poses suggested, 'the novelist's pose as he-man adventurer at least began as a strategy for disarming his critics, to whose doubts and strictures he was preternaturally sensitive' (Schickel 116–17). The counter-personas of Margaret Atwood could not, admittedly, be more removed from those of Papa Hemingway, but in some ways her substitution of alternate visualizations fulfills that same purpose of pre-emptive critical strike. Clearly Atwood was aware of such an approach to literary celebrity. From a literary compatriot, Farley Mowat, she early learned that such personas could function as a protective cover. As she mused to Helen Slinger in 1976, 'Maybe I should do what Farley Mowat does – construct a public persona that has nothing really to do with him. But he sends it out and does his number, dancing on tables and whatnot, and everybody takes that as what he's really like. And he, himself, is not bothered' (6). These were some of the options open to Atwood when she first began to understand that her fame would have an effect on her everyday life; as it turns out, though, she resisted the Byronic overdramatized celebrity persona and opted, instead, for a combination of privacy protection and meta-critical interventions into her own celebrity image.

Both the comics and comments in interviews are examples of direct critical intervention, but there is another, less direct way in which Atwood re-enacts her own celebrity image: through her fiction. Critics have begun to discern this thread in Atwood's work; Susanne Becker, for instance, has briefly traced Atwood's wry play on her own celebrity in *Lady Oracle*, in the figure of the literary rising star Joan Foster, who is noted for her wild hair, no less. Of course, in *Lady Oracle* the play on celebrity identities is multilayered; witness Joan's opening exchange with the flamboyant performance artist the Royal Porcupine:

'Are you Lady Oracle?' he said.

'It's the name of my book,' I said.

'Terrific title,' he said. 'Terrible book. It's a left-over from the nineteenth century. I think it's a combination of Rod McKuen and Kahlil Gibran.'

'That's what my publisher thought too,' I said.

'I guess you're a publishing success,' he said. 'What's it like to be a successful bad writer?'

I was beginning to feel angry. 'Why don't you publish and find out?' I said.

'Hey,' he said, grinning, 'temper. You've got fantastic hair, anyway. Don't ever cut it off.' (240)

In one compact passage, Atwood skewers a number of assumptions about literary celebrities, markets, and criticism. Joan faces the age-old confusion between her writerly identity and a persona from one of her books (a critical muddle that Atwood has frequently critiqued). Next, she needs to defend herself from the sort of assumption that Bourdieu examines in his writings on literary value: the assumption that best-sellers rank lower in cultural capital and must therefore be seen as a sellout. All of this topped off with a nice dollop of condescending sexism, featuring – self-consciously – the physical feature that has defined the Atwoodian celebrity logo. As Joan Foster explains, her hair's 'length and color had been a sort of trademark. Every newspaper clipping, friendly or hostile, had mentioned it, in fact a lot of space had been devoted to it: hair in the female was regarded as more important than talent or the lack of it' (9). The self-conscious, satirical play with Atwood's own trademark is wickedly satisfying, but what is less often commented upon is Atwood's sophisticated take on the workings of literary celebrity in the marketplace. Becker comments that *Cat's Eye* 'explores notions of artistic celebrity on a more serious note' than *Lady Oracle* (36), but the comic flavour of the earlier book belies an utterly serious take on literary celebrity.

If *Lady Oracle* charts the rising star's initiation into the fame

game and its overdetermined concern with physical appearance, *Cat's Eye* is its coda. At the other side of a successful career,
painter Elaine Risley returns to Toronto to attend a retrospective of her works, and, like Joan Foster, she immediately feels put
on the spot because of her physical appearance. Entering the art
gallery, Elaine knows 'immediately that I should not have worn
this powder-blue jogging outfit. Powder blue is light-weight. I
should have worn nun black, Dracula-black, like all proper
female painters' (116). And Atwood plays satirically on her
often-remarked-upon diminutive height; to the observation of
the pretentious gallery curator, Charna, 'I thought you would be
different,' Elaine asks, 'Different how?' When Charna replies
'Bigger,' Elaine retorts: 'I am bigger' (117). The fetishistic hair
makes a return appearance, as it does in most of Atwood's satirical fictional personas; Elaine's 'self-portrait of sorts,' a painting
entitled *Cat's Eye*, is a portrait of the artist from the nose up: 'just
the upper half of the nose, the eyes looking outward, the fore-
head and the topping of hair.' In the mirror, though, 'the back
of my head is visible; but the hair is different, younger' (549–
50). In this novel, even the trademark hair is retrospective.

Atwood has continued to insert her celebrity persona into
her fiction, trademarks and all. In the cases of Joan and Elaine,
this correspondence is hardly surprising, since both are artist
figures, but in the case of *The Robber Bride* Atwood becomes
more slyly playful with her celebrity persona. In one of her comics devoted to hellish interview experiences, she shows herself
being asked by a doltish radio interviewer which one of the
characters from *The Robber Bride* is most like her. Sitting in her
black dress boots and hat, an unimpressed Atwood replies,
'Zenia.' At this, the interviewer forms a visual image of a gor-
geous, curvaceous Zenia and stammers his surprise at her
answer. For the interviewer, physical appearance is the sum and
limit of his interpretation of that character and, it follows, of
her author too. But as Atwood explained to Val Ross from the
Globe and Mail, 'Of course I'm Zenia-like. She's a liar. And what
do novelists do? They lie.' Ross then reports that 'Zenia is
crowned [with] a nimbus of wild hair, she says, as a way to pay

back the journalists who over the years have described the Atwood coiffure as "Medusa-like"' ('Playing' C2). In novel after novel, Atwood reproduces her own star image as performed satire, suggesting, along with Joan Foster, that literary celebrity is itself a species of performance.

I have described Atwood's performance and rehearsal of her own star image as both challenging and yet confirming her celebrity status, and in many ways her response to her celebrity is similarly fraught. I would describe Atwood's take on celebrity as distinctly uneasy and would furthermore theorize that this unease is part and parcel of celebrity as a concept and condition. It is persistently associated with her fame, whether that fame is constructed by others or, preemptively, by herself. Much of this unease has to do with the question, fully explored by David Marshall, of what kinds of power, if any, celebrities can be said to possess. Marshall admits that celebrity is 'a less definable form of power' operating 'in contemporary culture,' for it is not power in 'any overt political sense' (ix). In some senses, in fact, the celebrity inhabits power and powerlessness simultaneously and is ceaselessly buffeted back and forth between the two conditions. The celebrity is assumed to be significant. He or she utters things and is given cultural attention, whether that attention takes the form of respect or ridicule. At the same time, however, as Marshall puts it, 'the celebrity is viewed in the most antipathetic manner' (xi). What better case study in Canadian letters than Margaret Atwood, the simultaneously revered and resented literary star?

As regards power, this uneasy fame that both enables and undercuts finds expression in Atwood's own conflicted responses to her celebrity. On one hand, she is given, as we have seen, to modest, self-deprecating rebuttals of her fame, insisting that she is both identified and alienated by the label 'celebrity.' As she told CBC's *National Magazine*, a performance artist made a video in which he complained that Canada was disappointing because you could get on the subway and run into Margaret Atwood. As she joked, 'surely celebrities ought to be driving around in limousines and wearing white fox fur and doing Hol-

lywood things and what have we got, you know, Margaret
Atwood with her shopping bag. How dowdy' (CBC, National
Magazine). Not as dowdy as one might think. During the late
seventies and early eighties, around the time she published *Life
Before Man*, articles appeared in Canadian newspapers about
Atwood's (apparently) unseemly riding about in limousines. In
a piece that reeks of male defensiveness, Frank Jones of the *Toronto Star* quotes Atwood to the effect that 'I thought it was just
silly the first time I got into the limousine. But now I realize it's
so much easier for getting around (on the publicity tour) than
having to hail cabs all the time' (D1). What seems a fairly
straightforward matter of convenience gets built up, in Jones's
column (entitled 'Atwood Hits the Big Time: "A Limousine is so
much easier"') as part of his rant against the feminism of
Atwood and American writer Marge Piercy, with whom Atwood
was reading in Toronto. The accoutrements of fame, no matter
how convenient, are dangerous accessories for a writer to
adopt, and strategies of downplaying one's celebrity are, as a
result, risky because they do seem to disavow a celebrity that a
writer may, in some degree, possess.

Another means of downplaying literary fame is to contrast it
with its seemingly authentic version, fame in the entertainment
sector. As Atwood told an audience after having her novel *The
Handmaid's Tale* chosen as required reading for French students
qualifying as teachers, 'Anybody who has lived any length of
time at all knows that you can be very popular one year, then
not ... So it goes up and down like everything else, I don't think
it's quite as bad in literature as in the world of pop singing, but
there are fashions in these things and you just have to more or
less ignore them' (Spicer D11). Despite Atwood's attempts to
displace her renown onto cultural fields that are more predictably dominated by the celebrity phenomenon, observers insist
upon confirming Atwood's fame by having recourse to comparison with exactly those fields. She has been labelled, variously,
'like a rock star in Canada' (by her American editor Nan Talese
[Collison 100]); Canadian literature's Gordon Lightfoot (journalist Roy MacGregor in the 1970s [64]); and 'like the Rolling

Stones' (head of PR for her Swedish publisher [Ross, 'Atwood Industry' A6]). The uneasiness multiplies; fame for a literary producer needs both to be discounted as not really living up to the gold standard of celebrity set by the entertainment industries so that the writer can protect cultural capital, but it also needs to be established, justified by recourse to those very systems of celebrity value.

As I have suggested, the unease that dogs celebrities, whether literary or in other cultural venues, is endemic to the condition of celebrity itself. And the reason why that is so is the contradiction that lies at the heart of celebrity. In *Stars* Richard Dyer notes that the relation of the star to ideological contradiction 'may be one of displacement ... or the suppression of one half of the contradiction and the foregrounding of the other ... or else it may be that the star effects a "magic" reconciliation' (30). This is the aspect of Atwood's celebrity unease that I want to examine. Whereas commentators on her stardom have focused on what they feel her star image means, and whom it might appeal to, I am interested in how aspects of that image may disclose a whole panoply of positions on various debates and issues circulating in culture. For instance, whereas in *The Postcolonial Exotic* Graham Huggan accounts for Atwood's celebrity by listing the positive associations that readers have found with Atwood (e.g., Atwood as feminist; Atwood as nationalist), I see those attributes as sites of contestation. For some readers, the association of Atwood with feminism is a powerful disabler of celebrity status, just to name one example that may be particularly familiar to teachers of Atwood's work.

Among the many ideologies that the star text Margaret Atwood may be working to manage or resolve is the relation between women and achievement. Her uncompromising honesty about women's achievements, including her own, has aroused equal measures of praise and disaffection. She has often spoken about how, when she began to think about a career as a writer in the 1950s, the predominant attitude towards women and writing was one of scepticism. Writing could be thought of as a viable pursuit for women only insofar as it could be reconciled with traditional, heterosexual domestic duties. That Atwood, after she gained success, refused to play this game and has been fairly unblushing about her own hard work and talent, both wins over feminist supporters and alienates audiences with more conservative views. It also foregrounds the contested area of women and achievement and puts it squarely in the public domain. Reflecting on her own growing celebrity in 1979, she observed that 'people still have a hard time coping with power of any kind in a woman, and power in a writer is uncanny anyway' (MacGregor 66).

This node of intersection between two sources of uneasy power – gender and creativity – is worth considering further, especially in the light of celebrity studies. As Richard Dyer points out, labour is one of the most hotly contested social values associated with celebrity, since so much of cinematic stardom became constructed through a fetishistic fixation on the stars as creatures of leisure. At the same time, though, filmmaking is an especially intensive form of collective work, and so the contradiction began and continues today to be felt between stardom as leisure and the excess of consumption and stardom as earned through labour and talent. Though writers would seem to be able to rest upon solid evidence of their labour in the form of the publication of their books, the issue remains a contested one in this field as well. Writers must deal with the residues of Romanticism and its legacy in the inspired poet-seer, a situation many authors can appreciate when they are faced with the perennial audience question at book readings: 'Where do you get your ideas?' Audiences have a difficult time dealing with the contradiction between writing as labour and writing as divinely inspired frenzy. And to add to the complications, cultural commentators wonder about the role of agents and publicity people in shaping a literary career; John Ayre, for instance, points to 'Publishers, publicists and agents such as Phoebe Larmore, who were very canny in exploiting Atwood's image in the 1970s – first as woodland wraith with *Surfacing* then as pre-Raphaelite muse' (D14). As a result, even a writer with as prodigious a publication list as Margaret Atwood seems compelled to insist upon her celebrity as the fruit of labour. On her Web site (www.owtoad.com), she lists a number of favourite quotations 'For Your Corkboard,' culminating in: '*Interviewer:* 'To what do you attribute your success? *Joan Sutherland:* 'Bloody hard work, Duckie!'

Along with defending the role of labour in her success, Atwood also finds herself managing the contradictions of markets and celebrity. Many articles point out that Atwood is an unusual marketing phenomenon, in that she is considered both a literary writer and a best seller. As Sharon Bambenicis, a fiction buyer for the World's Biggest Bookstore pointed out, 'Atwood sells in the Danielle Steel / John Grisham range for us,' which cannot be said for any other Canadian author (Horton 14). And although Steel's total sales world-wide are much larger than Atwood's 'the gap is narrowing,' according to Doubleday's vice-president of marketing (Horton 14). As Atwood herself once put it, 'I've definitely broken the sound barrier between literary and commercial' (Ross 'Atwood Industry' A6).

What this mixing of sales categories creates is unease. In interview after interview, Atwood is asked questions about her healthy sales, especially in the period of the early eighties, when American sales of *Life before Man* were quite robust and its reviews positive. And so she found herself on the defensive once again, having to excuse her success. To Geoff Hancock's question 'Are literary and commercial success compatible?' Atwood takes a position on the topic of symbolic and economic value: 'History has shown there's no predictable relationship between the two. You can be a very good writer like James Joyce, neglected all your life and poor as a church mouse. You can be a Melville and write a masterpiece and have everybody dump on it during your lifetime and not have it recognized until 100 years afterward. So I don't think there's any relationship between the two and I think it's a form of snobbery, both ways, to think that there is' (Hancock 30). Atwood's exceptions recall Bourdieu's reminder that some exclusive small-producers may not be esteemed and 'some box-office successes may be recognized, at last in some sectors of the field, as genuine art' (39). But these rules and exceptions do not obscure the main point that, regardless of whether these fields of culture operate this way, they are broadly *perceived* to do so. And so, a crossover up-market success like Atwood must continually manage the boundaries between art and commerce that she senses her public is policing.

One of the ways in which she does this bears striking resemblance to the way she sometimes manages the public's fixation on her physical appearance: modesty. In a number of interviews and profiles, she admits to having broken the 'sound barrier' between symbolic and economic capital, but she also muffles the sonic boom by downplaying her sales. As she hastens to point out to Geoff Hancock, though she's just described herself as successful, she is 'relatively – not absolutely – successful. We're not talking about *Jaws*. We're not even talking about *The World According to Garp*' (31), pulling out a couple of commercially successful literary products that would have resonated in 1980, when she made the remark. Sixteen years later, Atwood offered the same nuanced reading of her success, this time after the publication and success of *Alias Grace*; once again she follows up a comment on her success with the reminder that sales figures are relative. As her interviewer, Val Ross from the *Globe and Mail*, reassures readers, 'She understands where she sits on the bestseller spectrum. She may sell 10 times more copies than the average "serious" writer (about 15,000 copies in the United States), but her sales are only one-tenth those of, say, Stephen King.' Ross goes on to give particular details of King's annual income and sales of his most recent book ('Atwood Industry' A6). Once again, the boundaries between the commercial and the literary have been shaken up – only to be firmly redrawn, the better to discourage readers from assuming that Atwood is a mass-market best-seller.

Like the contradiction between labour and leisure, the tension between the public and private realms is often seen by theorists of celebrity as endemic to celebrity. As they explain, stardom offers a vexed space for the puzzling out of public and personal selves; to recall Marshall's point, celebrity is the very ground upon which we construct versions of selfhood under capitalism. Dyer puts essentially this same point in a slightly different manner: celebrity appears to offer the promise of reaching behind personas and icons to some form of real or authentic selfhood. Even historically, Richard deCordova argues, the invasion of privacy is a crucial precondition of stardom; as a phenomenon it arose around 1914 in the United States, as soon as 'the question of the player's existence outside his or her work in film became the primary focus of discourse. The private lives of the players were constituted as a site of knowledge and truth' (*Picture Personalities* 98). Atwood's grappling with this central contradiction of celebrity is apparent not only in the question of constructing a persona, as we have seen; it is in her skillful combination of revelation and secrecy in the construction of a self that is not reducible to either the personal or the public, but is a clever amalgamation of the two. As I mentioned, at one point Atwood briefly considered creating for herself a persona that would be so radically different from what she understands to be her real self that the latter would thereby be protected, as she argues Farley Mowat did in constructing a rowdy public persona. This possibility was only one of many that she contemplated, however, and these pondered positions, taken together, show exactly the sort of jockeying back and forth between revelation and secrecy that I've described. In the 1970s, in the first blush of Atwood's publishing success, complaints about her lack of privacy began to surface, but they did so largely as a result of her extending to journalists the sort of entrée into her private spaces that she has not felt able to offer since. As the question of her endangered privacy gained momentum in the next decade, she shifted gears in dealing with the media. It was then that she considered the advice that Mowat offered her, to create a diversionary persona. Around the same time, she toyed with the idea of giving up interviews altogether (Timson 60), an option that clearly had its drawbacks, as far as her peaceful coexistence with her publishers would be concerned. Then, in the early eighties, she lived briefly in London. As she explained to William French, 'it's just the price of fame. It was increasingly difficult to maintain pri-

vacy there [in Canada], to get any writing done without being
rude to people' ('I'm an Expert' E1). Clearly, the eighties were
a testing period, a time of trying out and evaluating different
ways of dealing with the persistent publicity/privacy dichotomy.
In the end, Atwood returned to Canada and cobbled together a
synthetic solution: to give interviews, but to conduct them on
her own terms and with a clear eye to protecting her boundaries and to policing both her persona and her privacy.

A prime example of this complicated combination of revelation and protection is Atwood's Web site. Like many such Web
sites, it offers the appearance of direct access, while also being a
tool to restrict access. The page entitled 'biography' is a bald list
of publications and awards; searchers hoping for juicy revela-
tions will not find them there. And the site includes some
frankly protective measures; supplicants for book blurbs, for
Atwood's opinion about their manuscript, for her help to find a
publisher all receive warnings that such help will not be forth-
coming. This is, of course, an eminently reasonable measure to
take, given the probable frequency of such demands. At the
same time, though, the site creates the impression of entrée, of
access. This is most cleverly suggested by the use of the icon of
Atwood's desk. Visitors to the site may click on any number of
drawers in that desk, and find various bits of information
(works on Atwood; excerpts from speeches; comics). This invi-
tational graphic seeks to balance out the regulatory, protective
aspects of other parts of the site. As with the carefully calibrated
slide show of personal pictures, Atwood ensures that if there is
going to be a visual spectacle, she is going to be in charge of the
light-and-sound show. In this respect, it offers a telling contrast
to the incident when Mazo de la Roche's desk was brazenly
rifled by a snoopy visiting journalist. As with her Web site desk
graphic, Atwood's persona takes control of her desk, agreeing
to open some personal spaces in a controlled atmosphere while
resolutely declaring her right to keep other drawers closed.

Surveying the wealth of media commentary on Atwood spanning almost forty years, I find that the unease that most consistently attaches itself to her fame has to do with nationality.

Recently, literary critics have picked up on this contradictory relationship that Atwood's fame and nationality bear to each other. A German scholar, Caroline Rosenthal, conducted a survey of responses to Atwood in various parts of the world, and she was frankly surprised to discover that the most lukewarm or even hostile critical comments came from Canada. As she noted, 'very few Canadian scholars praised Atwood's work but rather felt they had to put her achievements and success into perspective. Most of them seemed to be annoyed that Canadian literature is often identified with Atwood internationally, and that in most countries her fame has not promoted the study of other Canadian authors' (49–50). She concluded that Canada had a 'specific relationship to its most renowned author, who is proudly referred to as a superstar, on the one hand, and who is rejected for being one on the other' (43). As a scholar from Europe, Rosenthal had not, presumably, been a consistent consumer of the extensive media coverage of Atwood in Canada, but any reader of that coverage over nearly forty years could not have been surprised by these results.

Do Rosenthal's findings suggest a specifically Canadian response to celebrity? In her essay, she suggests that this might be the case: 'Whereas the US ritualize nationalism with their rhetoric of political speeches as well as in their treatment of national symbols and heroes, Canada ritualizes the nonreverence of national icons and the absence of a coherent national mythology' (50). In an interview in the *National Post* shortly after the publication of her essay, Rosenthal went further, proposing a specifically Canadian take on celebrity:

> Professor Rosenthal suggests that these findings are powerful indicators of the differences between the national psyches of the two countries, and help illustrate how Canada and the United States relate not only to their literature but to celebrity. While Canadians appear to have an innate sense of unease with fame and those who gain it internationally, she says, Americans quite simply assume that anyone famous, who sounds remotely like them, must be American' (Owens B6).

Atwood herself has characterized fame in Canada as 'uneasy'; as she explained to an Australian journalist reporting on her Booker win, 'We do like to feel that ... all should have prizes. So when one person is singled out, it's a slightly uneasy eminence' ('Atwood's Booker Win'). Though Rosenthal's and Atwood's analysis would appear to fit rather neatly into my argument about the relationship between Atwood's fame and her nationality as an uneasy one, I resist its assumptions about essential national character. I contend that the relationship between Atwood's fame and her Canadianness is fraught, but it does not necessarily follow that this unease constitutes a de facto Canadian characteristic that is distinct from its American counterpart. Instead, I argue, the unease that attaches itself to Atwood's fame in Canada is one manifestation of the contradiction between locality and globalism that attends celebrity in general.

Richard Dyer suggests that, rather than representing stable ideas, stars may represent values that are thought to be under threat or at issue. David Marshall, looking more closely at this idea, identifies several ideological debates or contradictions that find expression through the star. The one that is most applicable to this case of nationalism is the conflict between individuals and collectivities; he argues that celebrity has the 'capacity to house conceptions of individuality and simultaneously to embody or help embody "collective configurations" of the social world' (xi-xii). This is exactly what I see happening in the polarized responses to Atwood's fame in the Canadian media; commentators are staking out positions on the nature of individual and group achievement.

The media treatment of this question reached a climax when Atwood won the Booker Prize in 2000 for *The Blind Assassin;* on that occasion the familiar lines were drawn between celebration and sniping. In the months leading up to the announcement, the Canadian press was full of debate about the negative review that the novel had received in the *New York Times Book Review.* Such attention to one review (albeit in an influential – and non-Canadian – venue) seemed out of proportion, but that is in itself evidence of how entrenched the debate over Atwood's celebrity had become in Canada. When it was announced in November of that year that Atwood had won the Booker, several notices of her award made brief mention of that one negative review. What's more, coverage sometimes shaded into apologia; the *National Post*, for instance, followed up its lead coverage on her win with a commentary piece by Noah Richler rather dolorously entitled 'We Will be Made to Atone for This,' in which he opined that Atwood will be seen to have won for the wrong reasons, particularly because of her having been nominated three times before. His complaint had everything to do with the tension between individual and group achievement. Arguing that the Booker shortlist was weak, Richler claimed that there was actually a bumper crop of excellent Canadian fiction produced that year, but that the British judges could not perceive it. Again, individual achievement and the claims of the collectivity are set against each other. The fêting of Atwood is felt to devalue the cultural achievements of the group.

On the other hand, supporters of Atwood drew upon the sort of essentialized Canadian attitude to fame that Rosenthal gestures at. Heather Mallick, writing in the *Globe and Mail*, condemned what she sees as the 'absurdity of the Canadian middlebrow reaction to Margaret Atwood's big fat diamond of a novel *The Blind Assassin*, the typical cheese-paring response to her achievement of the Booker Prize,' which she played off against a warm British reception for Atwood's work. Atwood's Booker Prize became a litmus test for how Canadians see the role of individual achievement and its relation to national embodiment. Everyone taking positions on this question could be located somewhere on that spectrum that Rosenthal also describes, from those who celebrate her as a cosmopolitan artist who merely happens to be Canadian, to those who feel that her success somehow validates Canadian culture as a whole, to those who think she is overrated and undeserving of a fame that could better be spread out and shared by a wider range of cultural workers.

As for Atwood, she tends to share Rosenthal's theory of a distinctly Canadian attitude towards fame. At times of achievement (and therefore controversy) she has made this clear. In 1980 she told Geoff Hancock that 'I don't think Canada is used to the idea that Canadians can be good at anything' (31), drawing on the now familiar theory of the Canadian penchant for mediocrity. As she explicitly told Frank Jones, 'In Canada they want you to be mediocre – if you make it in the U.S. they always think you've sold out' (D1). Fêted in the United States at the time of the publication of *The Handmaid's Tale*, she told Canadian journalist Robert Collison that the Canadian response to the success of that novel in the American market proceeds from a 'pathological suspiciousness Canadians have about success' (Collison's paraphrase; 100). And some critics have taken up Atwood's lead: Robert Fulford, writing twenty-five years ago about the Canadian ressentiment issue, backed Atwood's public comments about a Canadian preference for mediocrity. Trying to make sense of why Canadians seem less than receptive to their foremost literary star, he asked a non-Canadian Atwood scholar with whom he was discussing this issue, how she would feel if her sister won the Nobel Prize. Her reply was 'shitty' ('Do Canadians' 12). Success of the individual amidst the collective family is necessarily fraught. But that dynamic arguably obtains anywhere, in any collectivity. As understandable as it may be for Atwood to seek some explanation for the uneven public response to her inside and outside her home country, essentialized concepts of national character offer a theoretically flawed way of accounting for the contradictions that are typical of the celebrity phenomenon.

In all of these instances, what we see is a series of attempts to freeze Atwood's star image in particular ways: critical observers have a stake in constructing a take on Atwood's celebrity. And the canny interventions that Atwood makes in that construction offer a way to unfreeze or frustrate such processes of reification. Because of that never-ending struggle to elude celebrity taxonomies, fame itself comes to be seen as a type of living death, a spectral presence that not only fills Atwood's non-fictional musings about her success but also her fictional portraits of literary and other forms of celebrity. In fact, looking back over At-

wood's fictional oeuvre, one can discern a persistent concern
with fame as a deathly spectre. In *Lady Oracle*, of course, this
theme is both pervasive and explicit; Joan Foster evidently finds
literary fame a condition worse than death; her faked suicide
becomes merely the metaphorical telling of her murder at the
hands of celebrity:

> I felt very visible. But it was as if someone with my name were out
> there in the real world, impersonating me, saying things I'd never
> said but which appeared in the newspapers, doing things for
> which I had to take the consequences: my dark twin, my fun-
> house-mirror reflection ... She wanted to kill me and take my
> place, and by the time she did this no one would notice the differ-
> ence because the media were in on the ploy, they were helping
> her. (19)

This passage uncannily echoes a number of comments Atwood
has made about the effects of fame. She has repeatedly been
drawn to the celebrity-twin notion; as she told a British journalist shortly after winning the Booker, fame 'is sort of like having a
twin who looks exactly like you, who is running around out of
control' (Viner). When one interview at a local restaurant
becomes an occasion for some intrusive Atwood-watching, she
mordantly observes, 'There's another Margaret Atwood running around out there that gets a lot of attention' (MacGregor
65). From the earlier perspective of *Lady Oracle*, fame sounds
eerily like a doppelganger haunting.

Later, in *Cat's Eye*, the memorialization that comes with fame
turns thoughts readily to death. Elaine Risley reads the positive
notices of her retrospective in the local Toronto paper, but all
she can see is the language of death: 'First the retrospective,
then the morgue,' she grimly notes (19). When she conducts
her own personal retrospective, strolling among her canvasses
on opening night, she has a moment where she realizes that
these paintings have both constructed her fame and consumed
her life, in an act of simultaneous giving of birth and succumb-
ing to death: 'I can no longer control these paintings, or tell

them what to mean. Whatever energy they have came out of
me. I'm what's left over' (551). First the retrospective, then the
morgue.

The morgue is exactly where Atwood's novel *Alias Grace* takes
us, and Susanne Becker is right to note that the tissue of fabrications, versions of truths, and lies is closely connected to fame:
'Atwood's exploration of the construction of celebrity – told in
a mixture of historical documents, newspaper reports, romanti-
cized accounts, and fictional plots – pointedly mirrors the workings of celebrity, sensationalism, and media hype in the late
twentieth century' (37). Grace Marks has achieved what Richard Ellmann, Oscar Wilde's biographer, once called 'fame's
wicked twin': notoriety (131). We are back to twinning, fame,
and destruction: a powerful constellation in the writing and
public persona of Margaret Atwood. In *Alias Grace* it is difficult
to say, for instance, whether the death scene is the one that is
investigated by the police or the one that Grace Marks lives out
as an infamous woman, both in captivity and after her release.
When she is about to be released from the Kingston Peniten-
tiary, she tells her friend Janet that because her 'story is too well
known' she is not likely to find employment anywhere; 'instead
of seeming my passport to liberty, the Pardon appeared to me
as a death sentence' (443–4). Like her fictional predecessor
and comic twin Joan Foster, Grace experiences fame (or
infamy) a species of death in life.

Because of this persistent twinning of famous lives and death,
I want to bring this chapter to a close by offering an alternate
reading of Atwood's major statement on the writing life, *Negotiating with the Dead*. These essays, based on the William Empson
lectures that she delivered at Cambridge in 2000, contend that
all writing involves and responds to a fascination with mortality,
with descending into the realms of death and finding something of use to bring back to the surface (178). I argue, though,
that this volume is, if less obviously, a meditation on fame,
haunted by the deathly spectre that celebrity has become for
Atwood.

Very early in the book Atwood draws a distinction between

the writer as writer and the writer as public personality that
recalls comments she has made about her own fame. 'Pay no
attention to the facsimiles of the writer that appear on talk-
shows, in newspaper interviews and the like,' she warns. 'They
ought not to have anything to do with what goes on between
you, the reader, and the page you are reading, where an invisible hand has left you some marks to decipher' (125–6). Here
Atwood returns to her persistent conception of the writer as
double, as split personality, but this split is exacerbated by the
workings of celebrity. In her second essay, 'Duplicity,' Atwood
poses a question: What is the connection between these two
manifestations of the writer, 'the one who exists when no writing is going forward' and the 'other, more shadowy and altogether more equivocal personage who shares the same body,
and who, when no one is looking, takes it over and uses it to
commit the actual writing' (35)? Here Atwood mobilizes one of
her favourite discourses, that of the tale of horror; writing
becomes a verbal invasion of the body snatchers, and writing a
crime that is committed. Fame, which exacerbates that split
between public and private writer, is, in this dramatization, a
scene of death. Negotiating with the dead is more than an
archetypal descent into the realms of mortality and knowledge,
though for Atwood it is certainly and profoundly that. It also
means negotiating with the living death that is fame.

This seems a mordant note to sound in closing about a writer
who passionately and cleverly insinuates herself into the star-
making machinations of the literary and media worlds. That, of
course, is one of the most striking effects of celebrity: its persistent baggage of mortality, offered amid the promise of life's
bounty. Memorializations of the famous always carry with them
this note of the graveyard; as Atwood herself joked when she
was given her own star on the Canadian Walk of Fame in Toronto, 'Look at it from my point of view – the parks are all used
up. I'm not going to get a park when I croak. So I'll have a couple of inches of cement' (Flynn). And after having won the
Booker Prize, she mused, 'I think they're relieved they did this
before I toppled into the grave' (Alan Freeman R1). Even on

this subject, Atwood does not hesitate to name the difficult subject, intervening in constructions of her own deathly fame. Amid all of the contradictory, uneasy tensions that characterize her celebrity, from visualization to nationalism, and from labour and leisure to mortality, Atwood has shown herself more than willing to insinuate her own version of the narratives that make up her celebrity. An anecdote from a 1982 fundraising dinner for the Writer's Development Trust wryly dramatizes Atwood's capacity to construct alternate versions of her famous self; unable to be at this event because of an Australian lecture tour, Atwood decorated a large life-sized effigy, a 'Peggy doll' that was set up at the dinner. This famous twin, this parody of a public persona, had a tape hidden in her purse, on which was recorded the following half of her conversation: "'Oh, you're a novelist, too" (Pause). "Oh, I wouldn't really have time to do that right now. I'm writing my own novel"' (Righton 36). Funny, duplicitous, self-protective, caustic, and distinctly uneasy-making: Margaret Atwood's celebrity persona is a vivacious spectre.

4 Michael Ondaatje and the 'Twentieth-Century Game of Fame'

> This award is not about winners, but about writers, writers who are working away at home. Nobody ever writes a book in a pressed suit.
>
> Michael Ondaatje

So said Michael Ondaatje, probably uncomfortably attired in one such suit, when he won the Giller Prize for Canadian fiction in 2000. Like Margaret Atwood's metaphor about the two Margarets running around, one very publicly promoting her books and winning awards, the other unobtrusively living her private domestic life, Ondaatje's distinction between the writer as labourer and the writer in the pressed suit is a way of putting an increasingly public writer's life into perspective. Seven years earlier, *The English Patient* won the Booker Prize for Literature, and just four years after that, Anthony Minghella's film version of the novel received nine Academy Awards. Canonized by the literary and the mainstream film worlds alike, Ondaatje garnered a hybrid celebrity that no other Canadian writer has known. (Though there was much fanfare before the release of Volker Schlondorff's *The Handmaid's Tale*, the film was not a major commercial success. And the Mary Miles Minter version of Montgomery's *Anne of Green Gables* was released at a time when Hollywood films, however celebrated, did not carry with them the enormous global audience that they do today.) The 1997 Academy Awards ceremony was viewed by one billion peo-

ple in ninety-one countries (Goodman). In April 1999, Vintage
Canada announced that over 100,000 trade paperback – not
mass market – copies of *The English Patient* were in print (Toller
14). By March 2002, 1.3 million copies of the book had been
sold in paperback alone (Lamey A2). In that same year, Canadian readers went on a buying spree for Ondaatje's earlier
novel *In the Skin of a Lion*. Voted the winner of CBC Radio's
'Canada Reads' contest, the book vaulted to number one on the
Globe and Mail's best-seller list. After the announcement, booksellers sold more copies of the book in two weeks than they had
during the previous year. Such figures mean that Ondaatje
inhabits the same intermediate position as Atwood, somewhere
between literary success and mass-market best-seller; as Leyla
Aker, an editorial assistant at Knopf described sales of *The
English Patient*, 'It's not as big as Michael Crichton, but it's bigger than almost anything else. For a work of literary fiction, it's
pretty amazing' (Lamey A2).

In terms of production figures, Ondaatje's celebrity is comparable to Atwood's, but in many other respects it assumes its own
distinct form. I argue that although Ondaatje negotiates the
uneasy balance between private and public that Atwood does,
between private labour and the world of public appearances, in
his case that negotiation is complicated by the attractions that
the world of stars holds for him and in his created fictional
worlds. And unlike Atwood, whose public persona is a WASP
one, and therefore usually taken for granted in mainstream
media representations of her, Ondaatje's public persona is overdetermined by an exoticizing and eroticizing attention to his
ethnicity. Much of Ondaatje's response to these forms of celebrity is to reject and deny them, insisting upon his privacy in a
way that goes far beyond Atwood's self-protections, which, however sharply defined, coexist with a very active agenda of public
appearances and pronouncements on sundry subjects. Of
course, such a determined rejection of fame becomes part of
the very celebrity persona that Ondaatje is in flight from, a species of literary Garbo effect. The literary celebrity of Michael
Ondaatje poses the following questions: Can celebrity ever, suc-

cessfully, be negated? Or is it in the very nature of celebrity to consume its own negations?

Faced with a similar question about literary recluses such as J.D. Salinger and Thomas Pynchon, Joe Moran, in his study of American celebrity authors, *Star Authors*, rejects the explanation that celebrity is able to 'incorporate diverse and apparently unassimilable elements to its own ends' because the appeal of the recluse would seem to 'run counter to the perpetual impulse towards commodity production in monopoly capitalism' (55). He opts for the explanation, instead, that 'the appeal of such authors rests primarily in the ability of celebrity to critique itself from within' (55). But such critique is, in itself, an assimilation of contradictory elements. Also, the celebrity of the reclusive author is entirely in keeping with the logic of monopoly capitalism, in that it provides another instance of the increasing value of scarce commodities. In this case, publicity is in relatively short supply. Moran comes closer to the mark in observing that the market 'will not triumph in a straight-forward, mechanical way' in literary celebrity 'because cultural capital plays such a pivotal role' therein (57). These are exactly the commodities that are uneasily at play in Michael Ondaatje's secretive fame.

Although Ondaatje is depicted in media writings about him as being exceptional in his demand for privacy, he just represents a more explicit expression of the conflict between the forces of privacy and publicity, cultural capital and marketability. Again, the comparison with Atwood is instructive. Because Atwood has bowed to a great deal of public performance, her canny protection of her privacy tends to be downplayed; it is a form of regulation that is effective precisely because it often appears not to be at work. She is adept at manipulating the strings that ensure privacy while maintaining an air of seeming access. Ondaatje's desire for privacy, on the other hand, assumes a greater magnitude in media representations of him as a public author. Among the writers examined in this study, I have not seen as pervasive an obsession with privacy in the media's treatment of a writer. In account after account,

Ondaatje is cast as 'intensely private and notoriously shy' (Cecily Ross S16); 'aggressively silent' (Marchand G1); 'modest and self-effacing ... notoriously wary of interviews' (Houpt R1, R2). Val Ross of the *Globe and Mail,* who disclosed the terms of agreement of her interview with Ondaatje (must meet on 'neutral ground,' mustn't mention his older brother financier, Christopher Ondaatje, mustn't mention or contact Ondaatje's wife), referred to him as 'adamantly private, an enigmatic black box' ('Minefields' C1). Not surprisingly, she refers to those classic literary black boxes, Thomas Pynchon and J.D. Salinger, as do other journalists who have faced the challenge of publicly profiling this most private of Canadian writers (Prokosh). Even the lead coverage of Ondaatje's Booker win highlighted this issue, in a way that was not the case when Atwood won: the *Globe and Mail* opened its front-page coverage of the win, 'Michael Ondaatje, the soft-spoken and intensely private Canadian author ...' (Koring A1). And their interview with Ondaatje on that occasion specifically raised the question of fame as problematic: 'Mr. Ondaatje, who shuns the limelight, acknowledged that winning will mean "that I just have to protect myself even more"' (A2).

But although Ondaatje's wish for privacy is well nigh pathologized in these accounts, and he himself refers to it as a kind of paranoia in his discussion with Val Ross ('Minefields' C1), it is simply a more intense version of the paradox that attends any form of literary celebrity: those who gain cultural currency by privately creating worlds need to market those worlds in a commercial setting. And for some writers, that transition is a painful one. As Ondaatje told the *Winnipeg Free Press*'s Kevin Prokosh, 'I'm a secretive guy ... What has happened [with celebrity] is that you lose a sense of anonymity. I'm more easily recognized. I'd much rather be backstage organizing something than be on stage. That's a problem' (B3). Explaining to the *Globe and Mail*'s Simon Houpt why he could not really be a film director, he noted, 'You have to kind of perform in public, which I find very difficult to do' (R2). Ironically, what Ondaatje has performed in public has been, in fact, his intense desire for privacy;

headlines for newspaper and magazine profiles of him parade this obsession: 'Spotlight Bothersome for Novelist' (Prokosh); 'Fame's Breath Hot on Ondaatje' (Cecily Ross); 'Aggressively Silent Michael Ondaatje' (Marchand); 'Ondaatje Learns to Deal with the Fame Bestowed by Oscar' (Ratliff); and 'Coming Through Success' (Italie), which plays on the title of Ondaatje's 1976 novel, *Coming Through Slaughter*, to place celebrity in a mordant key.

Such overwhelming attention to Ondaatje's struggle with his fame tends to render even the most typical instance of writerly privacy-seeking pathological. For instance, in a number of these media profiles, readers are told about his putatively secretive writing practices. *Maclean's*, naming him to their Honour Roll for 2000, divulges that 'he writes in secret, redrafting his novels in an opaque scrawl, and telling no one what they are about, not even his wife, until they are done' (Johnson 67). To a certain extent, Ondaatje helps to sustain this cloak-and-dagger image of his labour; as he explained in converstion with Atom Egoyan, 'When I'm writing a book – that usually takes about five or six years – it is a very private process. It's a secret and that's how it builds – in secret. And to have to tell someone what the book is about, even roughly, is kind of a problem for me' (Ondaatje and Egoyan D6). In interviews, he has spoken about that moment when he finally does let a few friends or family members into his work, asking for their feedback. As he told Jon Pearce back in 1980, 'Once that process is finished – the actual writing of the book into a first official draft – I give it to my wife and three or four friends who look at it and I listen to them and get their reactions' (141). This is the process that media accounts of Ondaatje romanticize as secretive, but what is striking about it is how unremarkable it is among writers in general. Many writers will decline to discuss works in progress, and many will not even show them to immediate family members. (Margaret Atwood, for instance, once experimented with exchanging work with her partner, writer Graeme Gibson, but, as they explain in Michael Rubbo's film *Once in August*, they abandoned the idea, because they feel that family members should not be put in the position to have to offer critical commentary but, instead, should be there primarily to offer support.) So this practice is hardly unusual in the writing world, but because the star profile of Michael Ondaatje features a near-Masonic secrecy, this routine practice becomes adapted to the dimensions of that legend.

Where Ondaatje is more justifiably described as private, however, is in his general conception of the writer. Indeed, he basically objects to the very concept that this study is devoted to analysing: the literary celebrity. As he has explained on several occasions, he is wary of any publicity that would constitute a means of interpreting the texts that he produces. This is how he justified his privacy ground rules for interviews to Val Ross: 'Privacy is essential. I've seen a lot of writers being interpreted by their personalities – Ginsberg, Layton, serious writers turned into personas' ('Minefields' C1). Accordingly, when Ondaatje wrote a critical analysis of one of Canadian literature's most unquestionable celebrities, Leonard Cohen, he warned readers early on that he would discuss the works, not the 'public personality,' 'because nothing is more irritating than to have your work translated by your life' (qtd. Finkle 93). Some of this approach could be attributed to Ondaatje's training in modernist aesthetics and his coming of age during a period of fierce reaction against biographical criticism in North America, but some of it is arguably rooted in his stated antipathy towards celebrity itself.

This is only half the story, however. If one looks closer at Ondaatje's quest for privacy, it belies a much more complicated relation to celebrity than the public Garbo persona would suggest. Even the same story about a public moment in Ondaatje's career can be narrated by him from strikingly different stances. For example, in relating the episode when, early in his career, *The Collected Works of Billy the Kid* won a Governor General's Award for poetry, and the by-then aged former prime minister John Diefenbaker rose up in anger at the awarding of the honour to what he considered a filthy book, Ondaatje often jokes that Diefenbaker did him, a young and still relatively unknown poet, a big favour: 'He hated it and thought it was outrageous and disgraceful that it had won the award. So he gave a press conference and suddenly my name was plastered on front pages. It was the nicest thing he could have done for me' (Gefen D3). Compare this to another telling of the same incident, which begins from roughly the same perspective but veers towards a more celebrity-shy stance: "Only about eight people had bought the book, so it was quite sweet in some way for him to read it ... I wasn't so upset by him disliking the book, but it put me in a tailspin about being semi-known. Even on a small scale, it was difficult not to be self-conscious about being a writer' (Ratliff G4). The first narration was from 1990, three years before the publication of *The English Patient;* the second response was offered in 1997, the week after the Academy Awards ceremony that understandably made Ondaatje's stance on celebrity and privacy a much more wary one.

Another redirection of attitudes about public personas of the writer came about through the making of Minghella's film *The English Patient*. Initially Ondaatje, as one might expect, shied away from getting involved in any of the publicity for the film. Just before the film was released, Derek Finkle reported that 'although Ondaatje was consulted on Minghella's screenplay and visited the set in both Italy and Tunisia, the film's publicist said that he had expressed little desire to attach himself to the project's publicity machine' (93). And yet, in the days and weeks to come, that would turn out to be not at all the case; Ondaatje did participate, to a surprising degree, in promoting the film. Typically, one might expect that even the most atten- tion-loving author might not have a strong public profile when his or her book is adapted to film; often, once the publication rights have been sold, authors have little input into the process. The visibility of Ondaatje throughout the promotion process seems to have surprised many observers; as Liam Lacey, the *Globe and Mail*'s film critic noted, 'Ondaatje, reputed to be shy of interviews, cheerfully made himself available for the round- table ritual of American press junkets' (C4). Promotional tours took him to several continents, and he and Minghella also did an immensely successful reading tour, reading, in turns, scenes from the novel and from the screenplay. This apparent change of attitude is partly due to the unexpectedly warm working relationship that Ondaatje formed with Minghella and others working on the film; Ondaatje has had, after all, a long-standing interest in film narratives and editing, evidenced by his recent book *The Conversations,* a collection of discussions with the widely respected film editor Walter Murch. In contrast to these positive collaborations, he has commented that, when the Shakespearean Festival in Stratford, Ontario, adapted his *Collected Works of Billy the Kid* for the stage, he was not welcomed or made to feel part of the artistic process at all (Gerstel D1). Still, at the very moment when the newspapers were full of descriptions of Ondaatje's legendary private, shy nature, he was actively and enthusiastically promoting the film that would bring his name to a whole new, mass audience.

This irony signals not hypocrisy but complexity. Though some commentators have suggested that Ondaatje's bid for privacy is self-interested, it merely signals the difficulty of conceptualizing the writer as a private citizen, at least in this culture at this moment. Derek Finkle suggests that 'the care with which Ondaatje avoids the CanLit bogeyman [i.e., publicity in Canada] may have less to do with the author's shyness than it does with his literary ambitions' (138). Finkle interviews Ondaatje critic Sam Solecki, whose musings run along a similar line: Ondaatje may be avoiding the ready trade in personal information that goes on in the Canadian literary world because he nurtures ambitions of international literary fame. As Solecki puts it, in appropriate celebrity terms, 'There's that wonderful statement Richler wrote years ago: "World famous all over Canada." I think Ondaatje senses that he can, like the Sinatra song, "make it anywhere"' (138). But it is difficult to see how readily information of a personal sort would, in any practical sense, obstruct a more cosmopolitan celebrity. For that matter, Ondaatje has, in the years following the release of *The English Patient,* both novel and film, achieved that sort of celebrity abroad, and it has not had the least bit of influence on his fervent desire to protect his privacy. If anything, as he says, his efforts in that department have redoubled.

This is why Ondaatje can, at one moment, distance himself from the world of film promotion and the next moment find himself on a cross-continental promotional tour for a film; or why he can, at one moment, offer tongue-in-check thanks to the late prime minister Diefenbaker for promoting his book and, at another, muse about how threatening he found even that small measure of celebrity as a young writer. The writer exists on that fulcrum between solitude and audience; the workings of celebrity, with their built-in paradoxes of privacy and publicity, simply exacerbate that condition.

For all Ondaatje's observations about the destructiveness of fame (whether in interviews or in his writing), he is still, arguably, strongly attracted to aspects of celebrity. On a lighter note, for instance, he co-edited a collection of reminiscences of people's meetings with celebrities, entitled *Brushes with Greatness* (including an unlikely one of his own, with the 1970s television star Jack Lord of *Hawaii Five-O*). His poetry is filled with references to a personal pantheon of stars and heroes that straddles the worlds of elite art and mass culture: Wallace Stevens, Dashiell Hammett, Henri Rousseau, King Kong, Humphrey Bogart, Burt Lancaster, Billie Holiday. As the speaker in 'Tin Roof' exclaims, 'I was brought up on movies and song!' (*Cinnamon Peeler* 120), and reading through Ondaatje's writing, particularly the poetry, one senses the same is true of Ondaatje. When he interviewed the distinguished film editor Walter Murch, Ondaatje seemed surprised that Murch seemed not to be as familiar with a raft of older Hollywood movies as he, himself, was; as he commented in his introduction to the book, 'There are very few in Hollywood who could speak of Beethoven and bees and Rupert Sheldrake and astronomy and Guido d'Arezzo with such knowledge. In fact, it soon became clear that the one weak link in Walter's knowledge was film history. "I don't know enough about film history" is not a modest remark but a truthful one' (xiii). But although Ondaatje's forays into film may speak to his lifelong obsession with film and icons of the stage, this obsession is complicated; as observers have noticed, it is typical of Ondaatje that, although given access to Hollywood and European celebrities such as Ralph Fiennes and Juliette Binoche, he forms, instead, a fast friendship and working collaboration with a film editor such as Murch, whose work, though absolutely crucial to the artistic production of a film, tends to be carried out behind the scenes. To recall Ondaatje's own reflection, 'I'd much rather be backstage organizing something than be on stage' (Prokosh B3). So Ondaatje's involvement in film may signal some of his attraction to the world of celebrity, but it does so in only a complicated, sideways – or backstage – manner.

The same might be said of the way in which personal references are handled in his writing. Again, for all that Ondaatje argues in interviews that art works should be approached as formal artifact rather than as reflections of a writer's persona, several critics have seen the personal as very much an active presence in Ondaatje's writing, though the way they have explained this presence has changed over time. Sam Solecki, for instance, has analysed the figure of the self-destructive artist who creates out of the materials of his or her own life in Ondaatje's poetry and in *Coming Through Slaughter*. At times, though, this approach implicitly theorizes a relationship between the work and the author that is problematically transparent; Solecki writes that '*Coming Through Slaughter*, even granting that it is fiction and not autobiography or even confessional poetry, is the story of Michael Ondaatje' (32–3). At the end of this essay, Solecki draws back somewhat from this equivalence, arguing that Bolden and Ondaatje are not exact mirror images; Bolden's art leads, finally, to 'chaos, madness and silence' (44), whereas Ondaatje's art is one of control and order. Still, he concludes by reinstating the autobiographical pact: 'In writing about Bolden Ondaatje seems to have placed to rest an urgent idea or impulse that if acted upon could have only meant the end of his own art' (45). Stephen Scobie, in an article written around the same time, shortly after the publication of *Coming Through Slaughter*, takes a slightly different approach, but ends up at the same conclusion; Ondaatje, he argues, disrupts the fictional framework to make an appearance in the novel (in the passage where the narrator reflects, 'When he went mad he was the same age as I am now'), but the intense empathy that Ondaatje feels with Bolden must be tempered by a recognition of the differences between the two artists: 'The kind of artist that Ondaatje describes Buddy Bolden as being could not have created the structure that is *Coming Through Slaughter*' (20). Such a view downplays the paradox that the novel contemplates, of order within seeming disarray, but more important to my present purposes, it also forges, then denies, an autobiographical link. More recently, W.M. Verhoeven has dealt with this question of the self-referentiality of Ondaatje's work without getting mired in the autobiographical assumption: 'Ondaatje's fiction is uncomfortably wedged between the awareness that writing is essentially an act of self-creation and the realization that the self is unknowable and incommunicable. The work also lies between the unavoidable creation of a public, writer's self (as part of the communicative process involving author, text and reader) and the need to protect his private, "author's" self from being "immobilized" in the course of that process' (25). It is this sideways, middle space between the inevitable creation of a public persona and the self-conscious recoil from that process of celebrity-making that I, too, find at work in Ondaatje.

This space in between explains why, for example, Ondaatje can simultaneously claim to resist autobiographical treatments of writers' works and repeatedly claim that his works are all, in some sense or other, attempts to represent a self. In *Conversations* he remarks to Walter Murch that 'I think, many novels are self-portraits – or future self-portraits, self-explorations, even if the story is set in an alien situation' (128). Speaking more pointedly about his own work to Catherine Bush, he reflected, 'I suppose I've always found characters for my books who reflect my age and concerns at the time. In a way these are all self-portraits and possible fictional portraits' (Bush 241). Typically, Ondaatje would place great emphasis on the terms 'reflect' and 'fictional,' so this statement is light years away from critics who would undertake simplistic biographical-fictional match-ups between, for instance, Ondaatje's own marital history and the recurrence of adulterous affairs in fiction such as *The English Patient* and *Coming Through Slaughter* (Finkle 94; Jewinski qtd. in Goodman). Besides being, frankly, intrusive and of little critical value, these theories do not sufficiently deal with the paradox of self-creation and self-unknowability that Verhoeven identifies. In terms of celebrity, Ondaatje's self-references do not enlighten readers about autobiographical content as much as they meditate on the very project of projecting – and evading – public personas.

References to his own life have always been a part of Ondaatje's work, and from the beginning this double project of building and dispersing a subject has been at work. His early poetry is filled with largely unglossed references to family and friends. In *The Collected Works of Billy the Kid*, he used friends' names for some of his outlaws and eccentrics; the madman Livingstone, who breeds hounds into madness, for instance, is wryly named for a friend, Ken Livingstone. Friends such as Stuart and Sally MacKinnon, who also appear in the early poetry from *The Dainty Monsters*, pose for a photograph of supposed frontier folk in the *Collected Works*. And so on. In the case of *The Collected Works of Billy the Kid*, this self-referencing underscores the portrait of the West that Ondaatje creates, one that stresses community, webs of relationship (for example, the Chisum ranch), over the lone gun image of the West. In so doing, though, Ondaatje enlists the workings of a form of celebrity forging; friends and family become worthy of legend, as worthy as the publicly celebrated – or vilified – icons of the West. Such a negation of celebrity does not, however, erase celebrity; it merely shifts its objects, and much of Ondaatje's work, be it *In the Skin of a Lion* or *Anil's Ghost*, derives its political impact from shifting celebrity away from its usual recipients.

When celebrity attention has shifted to Ondaatje in recent years, it has done so in a way that is complicit with an exoticizing of his ethnicity. This has not been the case with Atwood or

with Shields, though both writers' public personas do involve a
complex relationship between nationality and celebrity. Even
so, when Margaret Atwood creates as WASP-conscious a novel as
Life before Man, with its Ukrainian-Canadian character Lesje
Green feeling so mystified, at times, by the workings of old
WASP Toronto, the ethnic identifier 'WASP' does not often figure in media representations of the literary celebrity Margaret
Atwood. This is entirely different for Ondaatje, who, ironically,
did not turn to writing about his country of birth, Sri Lanka, for
the most part, until mid-career. From the start, he has been
exoticized by the Canadian literary community, and that exoticism has been grafted onto his more recent celebrity image. In
a 1992 interview, for example, Eleanor Wachtel appears to put
Ondaatje on the defensive, asking him, in effect, to testify to his
Canadianness:

> EW: You don't write much about Canada, except for your last
> novel and some of your poetry. Does that say something about
> your sense of self here?
> MO: I think I write quite a lot about Canada. I don't write essays or
> portraits of Canada, but a lot of what I felt about the country went
> into *In the Skin of a Lion*, and most of my poetry is about the land-
> scape around me, the people and emotions around me. I don't
> sense that I'm avoiding it.
> EW: Do you feel Canadian?
> MO: I feel Canadian. As a writer I feel very Canadian. I became a
> writer here. ('Interview with Michael Ondaatje' 260)

Ondaatje shrewdly hints to Wachtel that he is, after all, a writer
of fictions, not of patriotic 'essays or portraits' of Canada. The
fact that the interview was originally carried out under the aegis
of CBC Radio may explain, in part, its determination to pursue
the national angle, but it is also typical of the way that both criticism and media at large have handled Ondaatje as a persona. A
blunter version of the same tendency appears in critic Martha
Butterfield's short article on that 'Canadian' novel of
Ondaatje's, *In the Skin of a Lion*. She does indeed see the novel

as a turn towards an authentic Canadianness, in a way that
leaves much of Ondaatje's other work exoticized and marginal-
ized: 'Arriving ten years after his brother, Michael Ondaatje has
lived in Canada for twenty-five years, writing of foreign landscapes, of Sri Lanka's palms and cinnamon, of American outlaws and unstable black mountains. He is an anomaly in the
Canadian literary tradition ... The content and perspective of
his writing have kept him an outsider. Until now' (163). Butterfield praises *In the Skin of a Lion* precisely because its Canadian
setting seems, to her, to demonstrate a more teutonic discipline
than those unruly, 'unstable,' 'foreign landscapes': 'Winter [as
depicted in the novel] forces Ondaatje to order the chaos that
is his vision of life to a more distilled, more ascetic, more northern if you like, form' (163). This geographical binary is all too
familiar to readers of Edward Said, with its playing off of East-
ern unruliness and Western (Northern) rationality.

From an entirely different political perspective, Arun
Mukherjee's now well-known criticism of *Running in the Family*
also assumes that Ondaatje's work is exotic or, to be more pre-
cise, is complicit in its exoticization. Fuelled by the sorts of critical reactions to the book that animate Butterfield and others,
Mukherjee also ends up blaming Ondaatje for exoticism: 'We
are repeatedly given paradisiacal images of flower gardens,
paddy fields, tea estates and forest reserves but no contemporary picture of Sri Lanka – which Ondaatje calls Ceylon –
emerges' (121). Such a critique reflects Timothy Brennan's
observation that 'the political-correctness debate itself, ... in its
distinction between phony and real third-world literature ...
allows one to discuss the issue of celebrity making in the literary
field as an issue about native informants' (*At Home* 41). In his
influential essay 'Cosmopolitans and Celebrities,' Brennan
argues that celebrity writers from the Third World become go-
betweens, producing a portrait of their home spaces for a global audience in a way that caters to that audience's expectations. This is essentially the theoretical root of Mukherjee's
criticism. Numerous critics have responded to Mukherjee's con-
tention that Ondaatje is, in essence, a celebrity native infor-

mant, some agreeing and more disagreeing, but what is germane to this study of celebrity is the question of whence the exoticizing proceeds: from readers and critics or in part from Ondaatje's text? This is the classic consumption/production dialectic of celebrity, and my own position falls more heavily on the forces of consumption rather than production, in this case. Graham Huggan asks essentially the same question when, in response to Mukherjee's critique and the critical debate that emerged from it, he asks, 'In consciously exoticizing the country of his birth, might not Ondaatje be doing it – and himself – a big disservice? The answer depends on the extent to which the book is seen as ironic. I want to argue here that the ironies in *Running in the Family* are conspicuous and that they derive from Ondaatje's sense of the impossibility of the autobiographical task.' The ironies that Huggan refers to include, for example, Ondaatje's self-positioning as both 'the foreigner' and 'the prodigal who hates the foreigner' (*Postcolonial Exotic* 65). We are back to the in-between place where I locate Ondaatje's celebrity: the knowledge that a self – in this case an exoticized self – is inevitably being constructed and the resistance to that act of constructing a celebrity self.

This critical debate swirled around the publication of *Running in the Family* in 1981 and the years following, but how does that conversation continue – or does it? – when Ondaatje wins the Booker and gains Hollywood's acclaim in the next decade? There is one argument that the excess of fame tended to cancel out Ondaatje's exoticized ethnicity, making him recuperable as a celebrity subject to a mainstream. This would seem to be the bearing of Tim Adams's review of *Anil's Ghost*, in which he argues that Ondaatje was previously marketed as 'an explorer of the post-colonial realities he inhabited as a result of his upbringing in Sri Lanka. But *The English Patient* changed all that; *The English Patient* has made Ondaatje a name that does not require any categorization.' Like Margaret Atwood or Carol Shields? In some forms of memorialization of his fame, this can be the case. *Maclean's*, for example, in placing Ondaatje on their Honour Roll of Canadians for 2000, engaged in exactly this sort of rhetoric: 'Ondaatje is our most international author. Quintessentially Canadian, his fiction deciphers identity and bleeds through borders' (Johnson 67). The claims of international and national fame are met; Ondaatje is both ours and the world's. So national claiming makes use of this refusal to categorize. But on balance, looking at media coverage of Ondaatje in the years following the publication of *The English Patient*, I would say that his image has remained resolutely exoticized. In a great deal of coverage of the making of the film *The English Patient*, the apparent exoticism of the film's locales and that of the novel's author are superimposed. The most embarrassing example of this was *Newsweek*'s coverage of the film, in which they noted that 'though he's lived in Toronto since 1962, Ondaatje retains an otherworldly air,' adding rather comically that 'born in Sri Lanka, he looks like a cross between Paul Newman and Zeus' (Power 82). And *Newsweek* comforts its readers, adding that, 'though Macedonians, blacks, cowboys and Sikhs crowd Ondaatje's stories, they are less about culture clash than culture melt' (82). From the American melting pot, the message is delivered to Canadian branch-plant readers of *Newsweek*: Ondaatje represents an exoticism – but a safe, policed one.

An aspect of this exoticizing of Ondaatje's works and of himself that academics have not really addressed is its erotic element. Journalists have been, not surprisingly, less reluctant to seize upon this dimension of Ondaatje's star persona. *Toronto Life* named Ondaatje one of Toronto's sexiest men. Noting this perhaps dubious honour, Keith Nickson, writing in *Books in Canada*, referred to what he calls Ondaatje's 'druglike effect on women' (7), and Derek Finkle, writing for *Saturday Night*, luxuriates in the subject: 'Ondaatje may be the closest thing we have to a literary sex symbol in Canada,' and he argues that this erotic appeal is part of 'his growing mystique' (92). It would be easy and understandable to dismiss this line of commentary as simply prurient junk journalism, but one picks up some hints of this prurience in other, more explicitly literary venues. Eleanor Wachtel, whose interviews do not usually involve grilling authors about their private lives, nevertheless asked Ondaatje,

'You choose romantic subjects to write about – the exoticism and romance of the desert, for instance. Your books, your poetry especially, are filled with love and romance. You yourself, I think, cut a romantic figure. Have you *ever* seen your life in romantic terms?' (261). Adopting momentarily the breathless prose of the teen magazine, Wachtel makes that slippery transition from textual exoticism to autobiography. In response, a patient Ondaatje disentangles the two: 'I don't see *my* life in romantic terms, but I want to see life in romantic terms. There is a difference between art and life, and this is the difficulty when one talks about the romantic or the exotic' (261). This is also the difficulty when one talks about literary celebrity: the created persona collects all sorts of attributes that readers discern in the writing; one thinks here of Margaret Atwood's Joan Foster in *Lady Oracle* being asked 'Are you Lady Oracle?' only to reply testily, 'It's the name of my book' (240).

It's curious that although literary critics of Ondaatje's works have energetically debated the charge of exoticism in his works, there has been little academic consideration of the exoticism and its concomitant eroticism, that attaches itself to his public persona. Belonging to a generation that had to distance itself from theories of authorial intent, many critics today shy away from even a distanced, theorized consideration of authorial personas as they are mobilized in the marketing of books. But any consideration of the question of exoticism and Michael Ondaatje's writing needs to contend with the fact that this is a writer who has also been, in his authorial persona as a public figure in Canada, both exoticized and eroticized as a literary celebrity. And the result of these processes has been a curiously double-edged canonization: Ondaatje is, at once, both welcomed into the pantheon of celebrated Canadian writers and subtly distanced from it, as an object of a gaze that continues to proclaim him 'an anomaly.'

The subject of celebrity that one finds played out in Ondaatje's works and the workings of celebrity in his own persona are crucially interwoven, so that rather than being set apart as separate objects of discussion, they are productively analysed together. This becomes clear when one marks the transitions in the way celebrity is represented in Ondaatje's works. As Lynette Hunter observes, across a wide range of Ondaatje's texts there is a common concern with 'the commodification of self necessary to fame and to all public heroes' (205). Initially, in much of the early to middle-period work, that commodification, fame, is primarily destructive. In Ondaatje's lyric 'I Have Seen Pictures of Great Stars,' from *The Collected Works of Billy the Kid*, the implosive white dwarfs suggest the volatility and tension of worldly 'stars,' a reading that critics such as Sam Solecki and Stephen Scobie have amply developed. In another early poem, 'Heron Rex,' the condition of being an icon, representative and recognized, is the road to madness:

> There are ways of going
> physically mad, physically
> mad when you perfect the mind
> where you sacrifice yourself for the race
> when you are the representative when you allow
> yourself to be paraded in the cages
> celebrity a razor in the body. (*Cinnamon Peeler* 36)

These are the 'burned out stars' Ondaatje writes of in 'White Dwarfs,' those 'who implode into silence / after parading in the sky' (*Cinnamon Peeler* 48), and Sam Solecki and Stephen Scobie have convincingly related them to the pervasive imagery of stars and fans in Ondaatje's definitive treatment of fame the destroyer, *Coming Through Slaughter*. In that novel, according to Lynette Hunter, 'The artist can become a hero by commodifying self, but may also have self commodified by the public and then need to engage with that other version' (206). This is exactly the in-between stance on celebrity as simultaneously persona-construction and resistance to persona that I have argued characterizes not only texts by Michael Ondaatje but the star text that is 'Michael Ondaatje.'

In his middle works, written during the years that Ondaatje himself was becoming, if uncomfortably, better known, there is an increased concern about privacy. In addition to the spectacular self-destruction or implosions of Ondaatje's white dwarf stars, he writes of the tiny quotidian losses of those who live their lives in public, 'parading in the sky.' We meet a series of inarticulate, private men who resist publicity, from the narrator of *Running in the Family*, who recognizes in his paternal line a 'sense of secrecy, the desire to be reclusive' (142), to Hazen Lewis, Patrick's father in *In the Skin of a Lion*, a man who strives to be 'as invisible as possible' (18) and whose sole public performances as a square dance caller are strangely 'taciturn' – 'the unemotional tongue,' thinks Patrick (19). Nicholas Temelcoff, who is 'famous on the bridge, a daredevil' (34), is also, strangely, 'seen as a recluse' (47). These men seem to form a fraternity of sorts, an assurance that even the truly remarkable can be located, can exist to some degree, in a zone of privacy and silence. Hazen Lewis, who 'did not teach his son anything, no legend, no base of theory' (18), has unconsciously offered instruction nevertheless: 'It was strange for Patrick to realize later that he had learned important things' from him (19). Increasingly, Ondaatje works to relocate cultural value in spaces that have not been marked out by public réclame; this is, after all, the basic project of *In the Skin of a Lion*, with its determined desire to find histories in corners darkened by time and neglect.

As Ondaatje deepens his awareness of the political in his writing, in works like *Handwriting*, he also recognizes that literary fame offers no protection against persecution. It is better for poets to operate in the darker corners:

> The poets wrote their stories on rock and leaf
> to celebrate the work of the day,
> the shadow pleasures of night.
> *Kanakara*, they said.
> *Tharu piri* ...
>
> They slept, famous in palace courtyards
> then hid within forests when they were hunted

for composing the arts of love and science
while there was war to celebrate.

They were revealed in their darknesses
– as if a torch were held above the night sea
exposing the bodies of fish –
and were killed and made more famous. (23)

We move, through Ondaatje's writings of celebrity, from spectacular destructions to private alternative celebrity, to the use-
lessness and political fickleness of literary fame. In these
sobering lines, we see that celebrity is still dangerous, still a
'razor in the body.'

Where we end up, in this journey through Ondaatje's writing,
as far as celebrity is concerned, is the growing tendency to see
celebrity as useless at best, harmful at worst. In *Anil's Ghost*, Anil
Tissera returns to Sri Lanka, which had been the scene of her
'early celebrity' as a competitive swimmer (11), but now she
wants more than anything else to abandon that celebrity, that
shadowy formerly famous self. But it pursues her; either she is
recalled as the swimmer or as the young woman who 'won the
scholarship to America' (25). What Ondaatje's novel reveals,
though, is how this form of celebrity both saves her life, for she
avoids Sarath's fate, and also implicates her in systems of
oppression. As we hear at the end of the novel, when it is time
to resurrect the Buddha statue and reconstruct it – a metaphor
for the building of a life in Sri Lanka in the teeth of civil unrest
– celebrities are useless: 'It was assumed that Ananda [the stone-
cutter] would be working under the authority and guidance of
foreign specialists but in the end these celebrities never came'
(301). Suddenly, celebrities are beside the point, unnecessary.
As Ondaatje explained to Atom Egoyan his decision not to
focus on politicians and generals in the novel, 'The West is
obsessed by celluloid stars and political or military figures. But
celebrating the unhistorical is one way to make a moral decision' (Ondaatje and Egoyan D6). Western celebrity, in this view,
celebrates a version of individualism that negates the subjectiv-

ity of others living elsewhere; as Gamini describes the ending of typical Western movies or novels about wars abroad, 'The American or the Englishman gets on a plane and leaves. That's it. The camera leaves with him ... The tired hero ... Go home. Write a book. Hit the circuit' (285–6). This is as striking a self-reference as the moment in *Coming Through Slaughter* when the narrator asks of Buddy Bolden, 'What was there in that, before I knew your nation your colour your age, that made me push my arm forward and spill it through the front of your mirror and clutch myself?' (134). And it is every bit as much a self-indictment as the declaration in *Running in the Family*, about Ondaatje being both the foreigner and the prodigal who hates the foreigner. Ondaatje, in his first novel after the brouhaha that accompanied *The English Patient*, book and movie, pens an indictment of the celebrity author and filmmaker. He cannot help but be a part of this tradition of the East as seen through Westernized eyes, but as Huggan argues about exoticism in *Running in the Family*, he is also conscious of his celebrity and its ultimate complicity.

It is fitting, then, that Ondaatje's own comments about celebrity strike the same mood in his later career. Celebrity is now not as much harmful as it is another realm entirely, one that is best ignored or denied. As he commented about the fame of his novel *The English Patient*, in some senses it means that the book inhabits a different realm altogether: 'I think what's happened is that *The English Patient* has become something that's not owned by me. It's in the hands of David Letterman now, which is really odd for someone who's a poet' (Ratliff G1). Note how Ondaatje, now celebrated for his novels and only secondarily thought of as a poet, reaffirms his commitment to small-scale cultural production. Like the poet figures of *Handwriting*, Ondaatje may be 'famous in palace courtyards,' in the world of large-scale production, but he would in some ways prefer to hide 'within forests.'

Another way to hide, for Ondaatje, is to reject the role of wise teacher or clairvoyant that some writers readily trade on. As he told Jon Pearce some years ago, he dislikes the mien of gifted seer that some writers adopt, as 'someone who supposedly "deserves" more, "knows" more, than the man on the street' (143) – as a celebrity, in a word. And one way that he resists that position of authority is to place himself continually in the role of student. As he told Catherine Bush during the time he was studying at Norman Jewison's Canadian Centre for Advanced Film Studies, 'Most of all, I like being in a position of learning. There's an unhealthy fate to people who get published and suddenly become representatives for this group or that group or become representatives of themselves, become an image' (244).

As I asked at the beginning of this chapter, can celebrity ever really be shucked off? Can Ondaatje un-'become an image'? Or do all of his attempts to resist, deflect, and ignore his celebrity end up merely forming yet another dimension of his star persona? It is true that Ondaatje has become Canada's literary exemplar of the Garbo mystique; no matter how firmly he declares his wish to 'be left alone,' the more this fuels talk of his enigmatic persona. And yet, as I've argued here, such a resistant approach to celebrity does not capture the complexity of Ondaatje's response to fame in his work or in his recorded comments. Ondaatje's literary celebrity is a contrary, hybrid affair, much like the inheritance by the persona-narrator of *Running in the Family* of both a public and a private self from the two branches of his family: 'I have been thinking that if she [Ondaatje's half-sister Susan] has Ondaatje blood and no Gratiaen blood then obviously it is from my mother's side that we got a sense of the dramatic, the tall stories, the determination to now and then hold the floor. The ham in us. While from my father, in spite of his temporary manic public behaviour, we got our sense of secrecy, the desire to be reclusive' (142). Even in the midst of a mass celebrity that no other Canadian author can quite lay claim to, these two lineages mix and do battle in Ondaatje's work and public life. Like his reclusive, famous English patient, Ondaatje too might well reflect, 'I was always a private man. It is difficult to realize I was so *discussed*' (255).

5 'Arriving Late as Always': The Literary Celebrity of Carol Shields

I very early formed the notion of being a writer, all the while knowing that this was impossible. Writers were like movie stars. Writers were men.

Carol Shields writing to Joan Thomas

Both the genre of literary celebrity and its gendered exclusions were all too apparent to a young Carol (Warner) Shields in the 1940s and 1950s. After all, she was born in Oak Park, Illinois, birthplace of a literary star who attained near-Hollywood-level fame and whose star text was aggressively gendered male: Ernest Hemingway. Literary celebrity must have seemed unrealistic to young Carol Warner for a whole array of reasons. But in her seventh and, unfortunately, last decade of life, she would attain the sort of literary celebrity in Canada that would leave reviewers reaching for comparisons with celluloid stardom; when she appeared in Toronto near the end of her life, in 2002, to attend the gala premiere of the musical version of her novel *Larry's Party,* the *Globe and Mail* seemed to describe a red-carpet event: 'Shields, looking fragile but elegant in a black velvet headdress and a red and black wool dress, arrived at the Bluma Appel Theatre. It was almost as if she were a Hollywood movie star rather than a Canadian writer' (Martin 'After the Party' R1). 'Almost as if': the tentative phrasing captures the supposed unseemliness of the comparison between literary and film celebrity. But as this study has suggested, this unseemliness is belied by the very real cultural leakage that occurs from one site of celebrity to another.

In the literary field of production, comparison with other writers is a customary way to parade a writer's renown, for example. In this way, literary celebrity is not that different, in essence, from other forms of fame. One popular way of establishing or upgrading a film or music celebrity's value on the marketplace, for instance, is to associate them with other stars in whose reflected star power they can bask. And so Britney Spears and Christina Aguilera publicly twisted tongues with Madonna at the 2003 MTV Video Music Awards, a move designed to prolong two young pop-music careers and resuscitate another one of earlier vintage. Movie starlets are often associated, right before the release of a new film, with older, A-list leading men, as the recent excessively public romance of Katie Holmes and Tom Cruise demonstrates. But in the world of literary production, though public tongue-wrestlings are not the usual publicity gambit, there is a process of consecration at work in the way that older, established writers may promote the work of an aspiring new writer.

In the case of Carol Shields, consecration takes another form. She represents a distinctive twist on the workings of Canadian literary celebrity. Unlike Atwood and Ondaatje, she came to prominence relatively late, publishing her first novel at the age of forty-one and not attaining literary celebrity until she was fifty-eight, with the 1993 publication of *The Stone Diaries*. The typical paradigm of star and novitiate does not quite fit her career path: by the time she came to celebrity she had already been mentoring young Canadian writers for some years. The trajectory of her career makes her an ideal case study to conclude my analysis of literary stardom in Canada: Does the literary renown of Carol Shields confirm or deny the existence of a paradigmatic Canadian literary celebrity?

On the whole, while Shields's career inevitably shares in some of the commonplaces and typical tensions of celebrity that I have been tracing in this study (ordinary versus special status,

'luck' versus hard work, the highlighting of issues of citizenship), it reminds us that there is no one profile or face of literary celebrity in Canada. Discourses of celebrity are notoriously
adaptive forces, and this study of Carol Shields will reveal just
how synthetic they are.

If Shields's celebrity did not depend on the traditional
expert–novitiate pattern, it is nevertheless true that when literary celebrity is heralded, it is often done by constructing a
celebrity context for the newly successful. Writers who succeed
on a grand scale are understood to have joined a pantheon of
canonized writers. When a very ill Carol Shields was celebrated
by her fellow writers in 2002, the *Globe and Mail* reported that
'an all-star cast of Canadian authors pays tribute to Carol
Shields.' And those all-stars featured the other two subjects of
my case studies; as the journalist Ray Conlogue noted, 'a large
part of the pantheon of Canadian writers, including Margaret
Atwood and Michael Ondaatje, was on hand to read from
Shields's work and recollect their encounters with her' (R3).
The *National Post* listed almost the same pantheon: 'Atwood,
Ondaatje and Urquhart among speakers at tonight's event'
(Heer B6). And when Shields died of breast cancer in the summer of 2003, the same names rang out in eulogy: the *Globe and
Mail*'s front-page coverage of her passing noted that 'only Margaret Atwood, Alice Munro and perhaps Michael Ondaatje
matched or exceeded her clout beyond Canada's borders'
(James Adams A1). In its extensive coverage further on in that
day's edition, the *Globe* reprinted a partial text of the speech
that Ondaatje had delivered at the tribute to Shields a year earlier. So it is clear that, in terms of the case studies of literary
celebrity in Canada that I have examined, though Atwood,
Ondaatje, and Shields are not by any means an exclusive group
of Canadian stars, they do function as a group whose celebrity is
mutually sustaining.

When a writer wins prestigious prizes, as Carol Shields eventually did, capturing the Governor General's Award and, by virtue of her dual citizenship, a Pulitzer Prize for *The Stone Diaries*,
this contextual celebrity takes on a double focus; writers are

ranked with other Canadian literary celebrities and with the international superstars. Shields was well aware of this, as her parody of academic and literary stardom, *Swann: A Mystery*, amply demonstrates. Morton Jimroy, the oily, elephantine biographer, is determined to find echoes of Jane Austen and Emily Dickinson in Mary Swann's poetry, the better to catapult her to fame. As Mary Eagleton notes in her Bourdieusian reading of *Swann*, 'Though the evidence [of these connections] is spurious, the method Jimroy employs is common in the literary field. It is important to mention high-status literary associations' so that both the poet and the biographer can be "consecrated" (320). Compare Eagleton's observations with this passage from Edward Eden and Dee Goertz's introduction to their 2003 volume of essays, *Carol Shields, Narrative Hunger, and the Possibilities of Fiction:* 'We ... seek to establish Shields's place in the broader sweep of literary history. James Atlas's claim that "she is *our* Jane Austen" seems trite, but it helps us begin to locate Shields in the canon of world literature in English. Like Austen, Charlotte Brontë, George Eliot, and Henry James, Shields places a high priority on the interior life ...' (10). This collection, edited by American scholars, clearly seeks to recuperate Shields for that 'broader' (read: Anglo-American) 'sweep of literary history.' A collection of essays that appeared the same year as Eden and Goertz's, Neil Besner's *Carol Shields: The Arts of a Writing Life*, takes a diametrically opposed approach to this issue of celebrity consecration, seeking, instead, to canonize Shields as a regionalist, a Winnipegger whose writing was vitally empowered by her twenty years' experience of living in Manitoba. The collection is even dedicated to 'the people of Winnipeg,' and numerous Winnipeg writers, friends of Shields's, and academics explore the role that their city played in Shields's fiction. Perry Nodelman's essay, for instance, attends to the way in which his students at the University of Winnipeg responded to *The Republic of Love* and its rather unusual characterization of Winnipeg as a city of romance. These two collections replay the typical tension in celebrity between local and international ownership of the star.

In other, journalistic venues, this competition for ownership of Shields's celebrity had already made itself clear for some years. As early as 1977, after the publication of her first novel, *Small Ceremonies*, in 1976, an unnamed member of a larger publishing house that was outbid on publishing rights to the paperback edition, paid tribute to Shields in the press by saying 'I think she's better than Atwood' (Staton 19). By 1976, Atwood was the gold standard in Canadian literary celebrity, and the anonymous publisher instinctively knew that such a comparison could potentially bring a new, unrecognized name to the attention of readers. Some years later, just before *The Stone Diaries* won the Pulitzer, it won the American National Book Critics Circle Award, having already won the Governor General's Literary Award and the Manitoba Book of the Year and been nominated for the Booker. At this point, comparisons with Atwood resurfaced, as confirmation of the star-making process that was fully underway. 'I think she's nipping at her [Atwood's] heels,' joked the marketing manager for Shields's Canadian publisher, Random House (Rosborough, 'Award Expected' D8). After the Pulitzer, however, the terms of celebrity comparison changed. The overwhelming urge was to use this prestigious American award as a springboard for the sorts of comparisons that Eden and Goertz would eventually make in their book. As the proud title of the *Winnipeg Free Press*'s coverage of Shields's Pulitzer win proclaimed, 'Shields Belongs to History,' because the prize put her 'in some illustrious company ... Ernest Hemingway, William Faulkner, Norman Mailer and Margaret Mitchell' (Prokosh and Rosborough C8). A few days later, covering the city's warm welcome for its returning star (Shields was on a promotional tour in Minneapolis when the news of her win was announced), the *Free Press* balanced its earlier, internationalist coverage with a headline that featured more of a local boast: 'She's One of Ours' (Rosborough). The celebrity tug-of-war between the local and the international tends to appear at these moments of special consecration such as the winning of prizes beyond the national borders.

In that period when *The Stone Diaries* was picking up award after award, from the local to the international, another feature of Shields's star profile that was consistently highlighted was her late arrival at literary celebrity. In this respect, too, Shields's career complicates one of the assumptions frequently made about celebrity: its rapidity. Legends abound in cinema history about celebrities whose fame is somehow inborn, apparent from an early age. And yet literary celebrity often has to adjust and revise this discourse of celebrity, in order to accommodate an apprenticeship period that will justify the celebrity as the outcome of hard work. In the case of Carol Shields, both sides of the celebrity discourse are apparent; slow in coming, celebrity nevertheless is described in breathy terms as sudden, as a catapult or surge. For instance, the opening of the *Globe and Mail*'s lead story about her death melded the two discourses: 'International success came late to Carol Shields, but when it did, it came in great, lifting waves' (James Adams A1).

This need for the discourse to accommodate Shields's slow fame produces some complicated effects that are inflected by gender and region. The typical understanding of Shields's career path was well summed up by Nino Ricci, a Canadian writer whose youthful climb to literary celebrity was, ironically, perhaps too vertiginous: 'from someone doggedly working away for many years somewhat at the fringes of the Canadian literary establishment to Pulitzer Prize winner and international best-seller' (173). In 1989, sixteen years after the publication of her first novel, the feminist quarterly *Room of One's Own* published a special issue on Carol Shields that was motivated, in part, by a sense of unjust neglect. As Eleanor Wachtel wrote in her introduction to the issue, Shields's growing confidence in her writing is tinged with 'a slight resentment, that the work isn't better known' ('Introduction' 2). In the commentaries by both Ricci and Wachtel, Shields's location outside of the English-language publishing mecca of Toronto is glanced at, but so, too, is her frequent attention to the closely observed details of middle-class women's domestic lives. What may happen when one gives assent to this narrative of slow fame, however, is that one may end up reinscribing a sense of these variables – regionalism, femaleness – as marginal, as belonging to the fringes. For instance, when Shields herself spoke of her growing success in 1992, after the warm reception of *The Republic of Love*, soon to be dwarfed by the success of *The Stone Diaries*, she modestly characterized it as an aimless drift: 'I must have made compromises [in order to be a writer, a mother, and a wife], but it wasn't conscious ... I just drifted along.' The *Winnipeg Free Press*, running this profile, latched on to Shields's words and created the title 'You Get Braver': novelist, poet, prof, and mom Carol Shields 'just drifted along' to success' (Quattrin C25).

While this disarming of the notion of the headlong rush to celebrity is attributable partly to Shields's well-known modesty, its effects can be harmful, as Helen Buss argues in 'Abducting Mary and Carol: Reading Carol Shields's *Swann* and the Representation of the Writer through Theories of Biographical Recognition.' There, she argues that Shields is quite aware of media attempts to recuperate her as a 'mom' as well as a 'novelist, poet' and 'prof'; that is, Shields 'shows herself very aware of the trap of being judged wanting by both "erotic" and "ambitious" plots [of narratives of women's literary success], and tactically steers the representation of her subjectivity between the two in an attempt to avoid abduction by either' (436). Drawing upon both Shields's representation in the media (the only sustained critical attempt to do this) and her representation of the biographical abduction of poet Mary Swann in *Swann*, Buss makes a convincing case, though in media representations of Shields I have witnessed more of the steering away from the plot of ambition to the plot of the domestic than vice versa. Shields consistently deflects claims about her success onto the domestic private realm, claiming, that even after winning the Pulitzer, she still 'stirs the porridge in the morning' (Andrews C1), revealing that when she received news of her Booker nomination she and her husband were 'just about to go out and buy some yogurt,' and confiding to a Winnipeg journalist her recipe for handling the storm of acclaim unleashed by *The Stone Diaries*: 'Yesterday I vacuumed. I found it just the right thing to do ... Today I ironed' (Rosborough, 'She's One of Ours' D8).

Part of this deflection is, no doubt, rooted in a reaction against the Hemingwayesque bravado that Shields was well acquainted with from a young age. She commented that her fame sickened her in some ways: 'Just listening to yourself blathering on induces a certain amount of self-loathing' (Turbide 'Masculine Maze' 82). But the danger of even this well-intentioned modesty is that it becomes reproduced, by media commentators, in ways that tend to confirm a reductively gendered portrait of the female writer. And so, following Shields's lead, journalist Carl Honoré notes of Shields that 'with her grey cardigan and mild manner, you can imagine her slipping on an apron to bake cookies' (D12). Jan Moir of the *Daily Telegraph* similarly re-creates Shields as a domestic goddess: 'Carol potters around the kitchen, chatting with the welcoming disposition of one who might drop everything at any minute to whisk up a batch of hot scones' (ES2). But, as Buss objects, such attention to the domestic plot runs the 'danger of placing the literary accomplishment in the discursive category of hobby or pastime' (437).

In *Swann*, Shields brings the representations of slow and sudden fame into direct conflict with each other, leaving no doubt as to their gendered associations in the literary field. Morton Jimroy reflects that his biographical subject, Mary Swann, 'was about to become famous at last, a woman who a few years ago, balanced on a thimbleful of praise. And when she was killed in the winter of 1965, there was hardly a person in the world who recognized her for the rarity she was' (104–5). Clearly Jimroy, like all of the academics in Shields's satirical novel, considers himself one of the perceptive few who did recognize Swann's talent, and, as a celebrated male biographer, he also feels empowered to augment the paltry, feminized 'thimbleful of praise' that has attended her slow ascent to fame. But in order for her to become, in Jimroy's mind, worthy of his biographical attentions, he needs to revise the narrative of her slow fame, the better to emphasize his power to consecrate, and so, at the Swann symposium, he sings a very different tune about the speed of her renown: 'Mary Swann is in a most peculiar position. As a literary figure, I mean. She has only recently been discovered and her star ... as they say, has risen very quickly. Too soon, for example, for her book to have been reprinted' (380). We are back to the melded discourse that was cobbled together to sum up Shields's career after her death – 'International success came late to Carol Shields, but when it did, it came in great, lifting waves.' In a manner like that of the academic Morton Jimroy, clearly uncomfortable in drawing upon the discourse of popular Hollywood ('her star ... as they say'), literary celebrity needs to modify screen celebrity's emphasis on sudden discovery, the better to protect the notions of apprenticeship, labour, and the academy's power to canonize.

In her last novel, Shields allows a living author to comment directly and satirically on the strange rewriting of a slow but successful career path. In the closing pages of *Unless*, we hear that Reta Winters undergoes a form of renaissance, thanks to a somewhat belated academic appreciation. Until this point, Winters, like Swann, has laboured with only a 'thimbleful of praise' until a Dr Charles Casey, an 'octogenarian dean of humanities' analyses her first novel in the *Yale Review*: 'The subversive insights of the novel had not been grasped, it seems, by its original reviewers two years ago. A correction is in order. What was simple is now seen as subtle' (318). Reta is under no misapprehensions as to the marketing implications of this sudden fame: Casey will provide a blurb for the sequel to that first novel, and his name will 'be printed in the same size type as the name Reta Winters' (318–19). A male academic with considerable institutional authority shares the authorship – and hence the celebrity – of Reta Winters. And in the wry, satiric voice of Winters, this supposedly sudden rise to fame creates an Atwoodian duplicity, a split consciousness: 'And I've noticed something else: Professor Casey's clever perspective has caused a part of my mind to fly up to the box-room skylight, from whence it looks down on me, mockingly' (319). Knowing the labour that has produced her slow fame, Reta must now survey, sardonically, her famous twin: the celebrity writer who has suddenly been 'discovered.'

These competing discourses of slow and fast fame are caught

up in the familiar idea of celebrity as a matter of luck. And 'luck' must be one of the most frequent words uttered in the novels and interviews of Carol Shields, though it is filled with as much ambiguity and shades of meaning as it is in celebrity discourse in general. As Richard Dyer notes, the concept of celebrity 'tries to orchestrate several contradictory elements: that ordinariness is the hallmark of the star; that the system rewards talent and "specialness"; that luck, "breaks," which may happen to anyone typify the career of the star; and that hard work and professionalism are necessary for stardom' (*Stars* 42). Media representations of Carol Shields abound in these same contradictions; Lesley Hughes's 1996 profile of Shields for *Chatelaine* contains all of them. Next to an exploration of how much the concept of work means to Shields, and how proud she was when she obtained her first office at the University of Winnipeg, Hughes situates, without explanation, luck as a foundation of Shields's success: 'she's leading a life much of humanity would dream about. Besides the literary acclaim, there's a happy 38-year marriage to a man who still adores her; five interesting children to whom she is close; a summer home in the French countryside' (113). Helen Buss criticizes this profile, above others, for reproducing a domestic portrait of Shields that downplays her literary work, and it is not difficult to see the justice of this criticism, given the proportion of domestic to professional detail in this passage alone. It also fully participates in a standard tradition of celebrity portraiture that tends to present luck and labour, coterminously, as prerequisites for stardom.

Shields at times seems to acquiesce in her domestication and at times redirects attention, as Buss argues, back to the professional. In an interview she did with the *Winnipeg Free Press* after being nominated for the Booker (and before winning the Pulitzer), entitled 'A Lucky Life,' Shields was asked the question, 'If Carol Shields was a character in one of your books, how would you describe her?' She replied, 'As someone who has had a lucky life' (Lyons 4). But when the interviewer pushes this discourse of lucky stardom further, asking her if she 'sees herself as glamorous' because of 'all that travel,' Shields puts on the

brakes with her hometown newspaper and reinstates the narrative of labour and celebrity deserved: 'actually, travelling is hard
work, especially that flight to Australia ... Once we're in France,
we don't travel that much. Otherwise I can't write when I'm
travelling. So travelling may not be the best thing for writers'
(4). With a readership of fellow Winnipeggers, Shields is particularly at pains to de-emphasize the celebrity aspects of her literary success; the celebrity, in no matter what field, needs to
calibrate very carefully the demands of the collectivity out of
which she has emerged.

One would think that this narrative of a lucky life would have
undergone some revision or even silencing when Shields's life
took a decided unlucky turn, with her diagnosis of terminal
breast cancer in 1998. But oddly enough, it persisted and was
adapted, even though to look back at that 1995 *Winnipeg Free
Press* 'lucky life' interview is painful, especially given its blurb: 'A
loving family, the right career, good health, Carol Shields says
she's got it all' (3). In a *New York Times Magazine* profile in 2002,
direly entitled 'Final Chapter,' the luck narrative persists,
though it mainly figures as a sombre prelude to Shields's post-
diagnosis reality. 'Fortune always seemed to be on her side,'
writes Maria Russo in that article. 'It all seems to have gone
remarkably smoothly, for which Shields is characteristically
quick to assign away the credit – she was lucky that marrying
Don at such a young age turned out to be such a good decision,
she benefitted from living in Winnipeg, a city that kept her far
from the pressures of the literary world, she was fortunate that
she found motherhood so "interesting"' (34). And yet, as with
so much else regarding Shields's literary celebrity, her final
novel, *Unless*, opens the previously closed doors on this concept
of luck, showing it to be duplicitous and disingenuous: 'Unless
you're lucky, unless you're healthy, fertile, unless you're loved
and fed, unless you're clear about your sexual direction, unless
you're offered what others are offered, you go down in the
darkness, down to despair' (224). In this final novel, Shields
takes the contradictory elements that have plagued not only
Reta Winters's life and career, but Shields's own celebrity

image, and reveals both her awareness of those contradictions and the anger unleashed by their persistence.

This is all the more arresting because, in the media's representation of her, Shields has consistently been depicted as gracious, modest – in short, unaffected by fame. And although this was true of Shields in many ways, it tends to obscure the extent of her celebrity and, thereby, of her achievement. As I have observed of an earlier generation of Canadian literary celebrities, the myth of the celebrity who is, paradoxically, untouched by fame is a powerful one. In Shields's case, it is a constant refrain, and I found that it was especially marked in Western Canadian assessments of her fame. Andris Taskans, editor of *Prairie Fire*, told the *Globe and Mail* that 'She's that rare thing – someone who has achieved the pinnacle of fame, at least in this country, but it hasn't gone to her head' (Renzetti D7). The *Vancouver Sun* ran a headline reading 'Pulitzer Prize Hasn't Changed Carol Shields' Life, She Says' (Andrews), and closer to home, the *Winnipeg Free Press* announced her Booker nomination with the headline 'Shields Takes Nomination in Stride' (Lyons). Fellow Winnipegger William Neville asserts, 'As her celebrity increased exponentially during the 1990s, this did not change; she was utterly unaffected by her own celebrity' (Neville 33). These are crucial claims for a local audience to make on 'their' celebrity; by apparently remaining unaffected by fame, the celebrity retains ties with the collectivity.

Going beyond the local reception of Shields's celebrity, another media commentator, Lesley Hughes, in her much-discussed *Chatelaine* profile of Shields, linked this characteristic of being unaffected by fame with another recurrent motif of Shields's fame: its late arrival. 'It dawns on me,' writes Hughes, 'that Carol Shields is utterly unaffected by her success at least in part because it took her so long' (115). And this, in turn, becomes proof of another trademark of the celebrity – her ordinariness: 'This, I think, is the secret of her feeling that she is ordinary, always among equals; she has been slow, always, to embrace the next of life's possibilities' (115). But although Hughes makes this chain of celebrity connections, from being unaffected by fame, to slow ascent, to ordinariness, it is capable of a much more sombre reading. Helen Buss roundly critiques this idea that being unaffected by fame is the unblemished virtue that we might think it is; in her view, it is just another way of diminishing women's achievements: 'The sense that a women writer must also be "average," that her achievements must appear incidental, that no amount of fame or money can possibly go to the heads of us wifely grandmothers is absolutely *de rigueur* in the discourse of *Chatelaine*' (437). And so it is in the discourse of women's literary celebrity, though some writers tend to comply with this emplotment, while others, like Atwood, resist it and are punished for doing so.

Though it seems clear that Shields was one of those who complied with this narrative, it is in the nature of celebrity texts to be various and contradictory, as has been evident in the images of Canadian literary stars such as Margaret Atwood and Michael Ondaatje. Accordingly, alongside this portrait that has emerged of Carol Shields as the modest, reticent, unwilling recipient of fame I want to place an angrier, more powerful star persona. Margaret Atwood, ever a canny reader of texts literary and otherwise, caught on to this often overlooked dimension of Shields, in the tribute that she paid to the ailing writer in Toronto in 2002. 'There has always been a dark thread [in Shields's fiction] and people have missed it' (Heer B6); 'the essence of Carol Shields's writing' is 'the iridescent, often hilarious surface of things, but also their ominous depths. The shimmering pleasure boat, all sails set, skimming giddily across the River Styx' ('Shields' D4). Atwood's point is easily sustained by a reading of the fiction, but it is also applicable to Shields's star image. Though scores of journalists have filled their profiles of Shields with the requisite nods to her humility and ladylike demeanour, a few have picked up her sharp, even sardonic awareness of this image even as it is in the process of being reproduced yet again. Leslie Forbes, interviewing Shields for the *Globe and Mail*, finds, to quote her article's title, 'more spice than nice' in her meeting with Shields. Shields confessed that she feels her own physical appearance contravenes the image of a successful woman author that audiences may bring with them to her readings: "'I'm too ordinary, middle-aged, no eccentric clothing or wild hair," she says, eyeing my own disheveled orange locks. "But it takes such a lot of energy to be eccentric'" (D2). Compared to the verbal joustings of Atwood in conversation with interviewers whom she finds either ill-prepared or rude, this may seem rather mild, but given Shields's legendary niceness, it creates a distinctly edgy effect.

In fictional terms, it recalls a disastrous interview scene early in *Unless*, in which Reta Winters, like Shields in my preceding example, departs from her customary and ingrained 'ladylike' niceness to offer several barbed comments about the way in which her celebrity persona takes shape in the media. 'I won't – not now – tuck the ends of my sentences into little licks of favour, and the next time a journalist pins me down with a personal question, trolling for information – Tell me, Mrs. Winters, how are you able to balance your family and professional life? – I will stare back with my newly practised stare' (30). In this razor-sharp satirical scene, Shields takes apart journalistic dissections of the woman writer in terms that signal the sort of self-conscious play on celebrity image that Atwood undertakes in *Lady Oracle* ('Mrs Winters with her familiar overbite' (30) – a clear reference to Shields's own appearance – is one journalistic phrase that Reta Winters understandably fumes over).

As these examples suggest, celebrity images do undergo change, particularly when, as in this case, a writer reaches a condition of celebrity that allows her to reflect self-consciously on her media image and to intervene to correct or revise that image. For Shields, unlike Atwood, that condition arrived late. While she was writing *Unless*, the knowledge that this would be her last novel may have strengthened her resolve to survey the way in which her image has been forged – and the gendered complications that have arisen from that image, with its motifs of niceness, modesty, unassumingness, and interest in the domestic. As Reta Winters angrily writes to a book reviewer who has listed her as one of several women writers who 'find universal verities in "small individual lives,"' women like Reta's daughter Norah may well feel that, as women, they are 'doomed to miniaturism' (249). Shields takes exactly the terms that have been used to praise or damn her fiction since the publication of her first book and unveils the anger that lies beneath her celebrity image as 'our' Jane Austen.

This dynamic, contestatory approach to star images reminds us that these personas are always open to revision and challenge, and yet, by and large, what has happened to the celebrity image of Carol Shields over four decades could be better described as a grafting of discourses. It is common to think of the ascent to stardom as creating an entirely different celebrity profile, but, as I have suggested, celebrity discourse is a notoriously adaptive phenomenon, winding itself around extant representations rather than marking a stark, sudden transformation. This is clearly the case with Carol Shields. Surveying her media image before and after *The Stone Diaries*, there is, in many ways, more continuity than disruption, which is surprising given the seemingly easy division between her pre-celebrity and post-celebrity careers. Earlier notices of Shields's career, like Gillian Welsh-Vickar's piece, 'A Fairly Unconventional Writer,' from 1988, just after the publication of *Swann*, draw a portrait of Shields as a relatively minor footnote in the nation's literature, a writer whose sales have been 'somewhat uneven.' Welsh-Vickar reports that Shields would 'like to improve' these figures, but she is 'still unsure how to do so.' However, this marketing conundrum is transformed into a positive quality by the end of the article; Shields is, according to Welsh-Vickar, unsure as to how to attract a large audience because, in part, she 'believes in writing what she feels, and will not be dictated to by trends or markets' (7). So, paradoxically, this lack of success becomes a marker of true devotion to Art. As Shields later commented to a journalist about those years, 'I was writing exactly what I wanted to write, not what would sell ... Writing wasn't a career. It was just what I did' (Hughes 115). This is precisely the cultural dynamic described by Bourdieu: the shunning of the workings of the marketplace and careerism by those who seek access to High Art status and cultural capital.

By contrast, a 1995 article by Diane Turbide, 'A Prairie Pulitzer,' from *Maclean's* seems to transport us to another universe: Shields's post-Pulitzer world. Instead of regretful glances at her uneven, modest sales, we have a full-blown statistics orgy. The senior editor at Viking Penguin describes plans for second and third printings of *The Stone Diaries*, totaling 80,000 copies, to make a final sum of 110,000 paperback copies in print. Turbide also reports on the status of various movie options, not only for *The Stone Diaries* but also for *Swann* and *The Republic of Love*. These reports – impressive sales figures, movie rights – are frequently assembled to confirm the status of a literary celebrity; articles on Atwood from the mid-eighties and on Ondaatje after *The English Patient* are much the same in this regard.

One would expect, therefore, to see a clean break with the previous media discourses about Shields's mid-list past. Yet, there is less evidence than one might expect of the sort of before-and-after transformation narrative that celebrity discourses so delight in. The discourse of ordinariness that marked the earlier accounts of Shields persists; it is just redeployed in the service of another narrative I have already noted: the tale of the celebrity who is unaffected by fame. Those features that dominate Shields's earlier media images – domesticity, family, the quotidian – are not, in the final event, erased by Shields's late-arriving success; they are integrated with the new celebrity discourse, the better to buttress and amplify it.

The metaphor of grafting seems particularly well suited to the celebrity of Carol Shields, for it is produced largely by a national graft: her move to Canada from the United States that allowed her, as a Canadian writer with dual citizenship, to qualify for the Pulitzer Prize that sealed her literary fame. As in the celebrity of Margaret Atwood and Michael Ondaatje, citizenship is crucially caught up in the literary fame of Carol Shields, though it figures differently in her case. For Atwood, there is the continuing struggle to be – *and* to resist being – the representative national literary icon, with all of the burdens and promotions that such a position entails. Ondaatje's citizenship is, after *The English Patient*, similarly bound up with issues of national pride and achievement, but it is also troubled by a continuing tendency to exoticize his Sri Lankan origins. For Shields, the citizenship issue is, like so much else about her celebrity image, a grafting, a nervous balancing of allegiances on the national as well as local fronts. Her cross-border fiction has challenged generic assumptions about what it means to be a Canadian or an American citizen; as she told Eleanor Wachtel, for instance, she was pressured by her publishers to change the setting for a story from Chicago to Toronto because they felt that the family relations were too gentle to be convincingly American. As Shields objected, 'That was ridiculous because I'd grown up in a family which was like that. My father had never fired a gun in his whole life.' And she added to Wachtel, 'The American reviews were better than the Canadian reviews' (34). The story recalls one of Canadian writer Timothy Findley setting his first novel, *The Last of the Crazy People*, in Toronto, and being told in reviews that his Southern U.S.-style tale of a child driven to violence by his repressed family was not realistic; that such things didn't happen in Toronto. Like Findley, Shields has shaken the verities of national character.

Because Shields is a transplanted American citizen whose success has been measured in terms of both her Canadian and her American citizenships, negotiating between these allegiances has been a matter requiring some diplomacy. The interview she did with the American journal *Contemporary Literature* is a perfect case in point. There, she tells the interviewer, Donna Krolik Hollenberg, that 'I see myself as a Canadian because I live here and have for forty years,' but during the course of the conversation Shields repeatedly jumps back and forth between Canadian and American allegiances. She quickly adds, for instance, 'But I have an American childhood and an American education. Today I carry two passports ... I have to say that I feel fortunate to have a foot on each side of the border' (352). The questions that Hollenberg poses to Shields presuppose American citizenship as a normative condition; as she rather leadingly inquires, 'How has your expatriation affected your career as a writer?' (352). Wishing to downplay the sometimes antagonistic relationship between the national neighbours, Shields once again diplomatically observes that 'I haven't ever had strong nationalistic feelings and indeed I feel uncomfortable in the presence of "patriotic" gestures' (352) – a gently worded, diplomatic response that, read a certain way, does make her reasons for living in Canada pointedly clear. But it's all couched in a denial of nationalist feelings. Responses to questions about the border driftings of her characters – Daisy in *The Stone Diaries* or Larry Weller in *Larry's Party* – feature this same, anxious balancing of nationalist allegiances; for instance, Shields asserts that 'I do worry about the Americanization of Canada,' only to soften this comment somewhat by adding 'At the same time, it feels natural to me to think of the North American "sphere"' (352–3). One could hardly imagine Margaret Atwood thus softening her critiques of American global interests, but then, on the other hand, she did not have a Pulitzer Prize to justify. This interview, carried out in 1998, evinces the complex tensions of the writer of dual citizenship, whose celebrity is facing claims from either side of the border.

If one compares Canadian interviews with Shields before American prizes like the Pulitzer or the National Book Critics Circle Award started to pour in, the critique of American literary circles is more pronounced, less apologetic. She told *Quill and Quire* in 1977, for instance, that even though her first novel was published by an American branch-plant publisher, it was first submitted to McClelland and Stewart, Oberon, and Anansi. And in the case of the latter two publishers, Shields received a warm and helpful response to her manuscript that she felt she would never have received south of the border. 'That's the nice thing about Canada,' remarked Shields on that occasion. 'They'd never write letters like that in the States' (Staton 18). Part of this split effect is the necessary diplomacy that any writer must employ when touring to promote a book, but in the case of Carol Shields, the duplicity is more pressing, more persistent once she attained celebrity in two national venues.

When Shields died, media representations tended to reproduce and reaffirm her diplomatic handling of the citizenship issue, but in so doing they also reproduced the tensions that this diplomacy involves and grows out of. The lead article for the *Globe and Mail* on the event of Shields's passing made sure to cover this binational aspect of Shields's career – hardly surprising, since the *Globe* has, in recent years, pursued an editorial policy that tends to favour closer ties between Canada and the United States. The article quoted fellow writer Jack Hodgins to the effect that 'you can't pin her down to one geographical location,' given her American origins, Canadian adult citizenship, and international fame. 'Maybe that's the reason,' Hodgins opined, 'that her work leapt over so many national boundaries' (James Adams A6). True though this patently is, it is revealing that this binational character of Shields's writing should have attracted special attention on the occasion of her death.

Cross-cutting this tension in Shields's celebrity is the local claim on her that I have already alluded to. In many ways, Shields's literary celebrity was a powerful arrow in Winnipeg's and the Canadian West's quiver when it came to assumptions about the cultural ascendancy of cities like Toronto and Montreal. And in the final stages of her career, after she had already moved to Victoria with her husband, Winnipeggers continued to exploit this source of cultural capital. As William Neville recalls, 'In due course Carol became a Canadian citizen. She was, in a very particular way, the epitome of the "good citizen" in Winnipeg where she accepted enthusiastically the opportunities and responsibilities that were the marks of citizenship' (Neville 34). These involved various civic duties that, for the most part, involved work of a less-than-glamorous or visible sort (serving on library boards, for example). As Neville narrates it, the city then exchanged for that good citizenship a number of benefits: her promotion to full professor at the University of Manitoba, the creation of the annual Carol Shields Winnipeg Book Award and, notably, 'election to the Winnipeg Citizens' Hall of Fame' (35). Of course, such benefits or tributes themselves act self-reflexively, to support the reputation of the city itself; that the Winnipeg Hall of Fame can boast an inductee who won both a Governor-General's Award and a Pulitzer Prize redounds to the fame of both parties.

This late testimony to the good citizenship of the famous city daughter is an important claim to make, when one considers the sense of loss that Winnipeggers felt in 1999, when Shields and her husband moved to Victoria. The event was even covered on the CBC Radio Web site under the title 'Acclaimed Writer Carol Shields Leaving Winnipeg' (Ringer). And a few months earlier, in the spring of 1999, when the Carol Shields Winnipeg Book Award was announced, it was done in the sad knowledge that two of the major aspects of the award title would soon be separated; as CBC Radio's Web site commented, 'Ironically, Carol Shields won't be living in the city much longer' (Crabb). So the award was a way to memorialize the relationship between Shields and Winnipeg, to give it a solidity that would ensure that her celebrity and that of the city would continue to be linked in Canadian literary people's minds. In a way, this, too, is one of the agendas of books like Besner's *Carol Shields: The Arts of a Writing Life:* to ensure that, in the midst of the binary debate about Shields's national citizenships set loose by the awarding of the Pulitzer, the claims of the local metropolis not be forgotten. His book also sends a clear message about the importance, to Winnipeg, of such a claim; as William Neville writes 'in his contribution to the volume, in Winnipeg, 'pride ... has always competed with an element of fragility and self-deprecation' (29). In the midst of globalizing media messages that typically privilege the metropolis or the superpower, the anxieties of a municipality like Winnipeg are understandable, as is their bid to cement their relationship with a famous writer, for reasons both cultural and economic.

In many ways, celebrity itself is, as I have suggested, a matter of laying claims to various forms of citizenship and capital, ways of defining allegiance to human environments and characteristics of various kinds. In the celebrity of Carol Shields, a number of typical markers of star status (international prize-winning, complicated issues of citizenship) are clearly at work, but so are some less expected features of a career that in many ways did not follow a script that young, aspiring writers may believe is the only road to success: quick recognition, life in a publishing metropolis, and a willingness to play, however cynically, the game of self-promotion. In her career, Shields defied all three of these recipes for success.

But what especially challenges typical representations of celebrity – mine included – is Shields's growing sense of self-consciousness about the terms and pitfalls of the way in which her celebrity self was represented at large. When I began work on this book, while Shields was still living and had not yet published *Unless*, I thought I knew all of the reasons why she would make a fitting complement to my other two celebrity case studies of Atwood and Ondaatje: a writer who experienced slow arrival to fame and was deemed regional and yet claimed by two nations, she seemed to embody some of the persistent concerns of celebrity – such as the enigmas of citizenship – and some of its exceptions. What I did not expect, though, was how self-conscious she would become about her own celebrity image, for I had, at the time, seen her as quietly acquiescing in the media's depiction of her as an unassuming, middle-class, heterosexual woman with an allegiance to domestic interests that have traditionally been marked as the province of women. The critique that surfaced in *Swann* was still more removed from self-conscious commentary; it is, for instance, not self-conscious in the way that Atwood's *Lady Oracle* is, with its knowing roman-à-clef nods to Canadian publishing people and institutions. Even knowing Helen Buss's argument that Shields tends to steer a tactical middle ground between professional and domestic narratives of her life, I tended to believe that the balance fell much more strongly on her reinforcing of the latter. And in mid-career, the evidence of media representations suggests that the emphasis did fall more strongly on the domestic, for the reasons I have explored. Shields, therefore, was to be something of a foil to Atwood and her career-long barbed satire and awareness about the conditions of literary stardom in general and her own media image in particular. But then *Unless* appeared and changed my perspective on Carol Shields the literary celebrity,

for at the end of her career, Shields summoned up the willingness – and the requisite anger – to set the record straight about
her awareness of her cooperation in the construction of her
image as a good female citizen. From the perspective of a long
and only recently celebrated career, Shields left readers in no
doubt that she was aware of the celebrity she had become and
its implications for the reductive gendering of women artists. As
her writer Reta Winters concludes one of her letters of exor-
cism, finally revealing her feelings about the way in which
women's creativity has been devalued, 'I am willing to blurt it all
out, if only to myself. Blurting is a form of bravery. I'm just
catching on to that fact. Arriving late, as always' (270). Arriving
late to success, arriving at the final destination of her own
career, Carol Shields took a hard look at her own celebrity
image, and found the bravery to 'blurt it all out.'

6 Walking the Walk: A Conclusion

From the flamboyant fabrications of Mazo de la Roche to the jealously guarded privacy of Michael Ondaatje, clearly there is no distinctive mode of Canadian literary celebrity. Still, given the tendency of celebrity studies to focus on the most contemporary of examples, it is instructive to see how many of the concerns and tensions involved in current Canadian literary celebrity have had a longer history in this country than one might suppose. Ondaatje's privacy finds its historical counterpart in the carefully protected domestic life of Stephen Leacock, and the canny interventions of Margaret Atwood into her own celebrity representations find their historical precedent in the clear-eyed awareness of L.M. Montgomery. But each celebrity performs his or her fame in a somewhat different key. Ondaatje's celebrity citizenship is complicated in a way that Atwood's is not by the widespread tendency to exoticize and eroticize his origins, his work, and his star persona. Shields's late-coming literary celebrity was marked by a public prurience about her domestic arrangements, as Margaret Atwood's has been, and yet Shields's public persona often adhered to the model of the good middle-class woman in a way that Atwood's has not. Indeed, it becomes clear that Atwood has, at numerous points in her career, been punished by the media, by literary reviewers and by readers, for not adhering to this image of the modestly accomplished domestic woman – for inhabiting her celebrity, for the most part, unapologetically.

For all that each of these literary celebrities performs these familiar celebrity tensions in a distinctive key, in popular parlance and in my own classroom experience teaching Canadian literary celebrity, we continue, as Canadians, to cling to the belief that there is something different – often something more simple, modest, or ennobling – about our approach to celebrity than what we perceive in the celebrity culture of the nation to our south. And yet a study such as this one reveals the flimsiness of such an assumption. In my classroom experience teaching topics such as Canadian women's literary celebrity, or famous Canadian women in the arts in general, I have found this belief in our national distrust of celebrity to be persistent and deep-rooted. In studying a work like Carol Shield's *Swann*, for instance, students are often tempted to see poor, neglected, murdered Mary Swann as a metaphor for Canadian celebrity culture and women's celebrity in general. According to this myth, Canadians, and Canadian women in particular, are more modest about their fame, less affected by it (in a way that media commentaries of Shields herself tended to depict her), and, therefore, more authentic and unspoiled as celebrities. As the growing body of theoretical work on celebrity has amply maintained, however, this claim of authenticity holds both powerful and unstable cultural currency. And in the context of this study, the strikingly different approaches to literary celebrity shown by women such as Mazo de la Roche, Margaret Atwood, and Carol Shields would seem to disperse any critical claim that there is a distinctive Canadian female performance of celebrity or that it is necessarily characterized by modesty or a lack of awareness.

Because this study has thrown into question these sorts of assumptions, I close my study of Canadian celebrity with a brief glance at an institution that seeks to define celebrity in a distinctively national key: the Canadian Walk of Fame. The Walk of Fame is a collection of concrete stars embossed with the names of Canadian notables set into several sidewalks in Toronto's Theatre District. Each June, several new stars are inducted into the Walk, nominated by members of the general public and chosen by a selection committee and board of directors. Over

time this ceremony has attracted increasing amounts of attention; currently, it is televised nationally each year on the CTV
network, and national newspapers cover the public announcement of that year's slate of inductees in March.

In relation to my study of literary celebrity, the first thing to
note about Canada's Walk of Fame is the relatively light emphasis placed on literary accomplishment. Given all of the publicity
that Canadians have heard about the increasing exportability of
our writers since the 1990s, literature is not given as prominent
a place on the Walk as one might expect. As of June 2006, out of
a roster of 101 notables who have been honoured with a star,
only three are writers. Of those three, only two, Margaret
Atwood and Timothy Findley, are or were primarily writers of
fiction. (The third was Pierre Berton.) As a trio, they are logical
choices, given the nationalist mandate of the Walk. Berton's
works, among them *The National Dream, The Last Spike,* and
Klondike, which are markedly middlebrow in their populist
retellings of Canadian history, constitute a classic exercise in
national myth-making. Findley's *The Wars* draws on documentary details of Canadian trench warfare at the Somme, but
besides his achievement in the writing of imaginative prose, one
can cite his substantial réclame outside of Canada. During the
later years of his life, he was awarded a Chevalier de l'Ordre des
Arts et des Lettres in France, where he and his partner, William
Whitehead, lived for half the year. His other place of residence,
Stratford, Ontario, gestures towards his participation in one of
Canada's most prized national cultural institutions, the Stratford Shakespearean Festival, where Findley worked as an actor
during its premier season. His award-winning CBC scripts for
The National Dream, which he co-wrote with Whitehead, based
on Pierre Berton's saga of the building of the Canadian Pacific
Railway, link Findley to yet another celebrated national institution – and to another Walk of Fame inductee. As far as Atwood
is concerned, her choice is obvious, for reasons already
explored in this study: a combination of immense international
success and years of being a spokesperson for various nationalist causes. So literary achievement, if it is going to be recognized

on Canada's Walk of Fame, apparently needs to work in the service of national self-definition.

This nationalist factor may help to preselect likely inductees, but the sparseness of representation of writers is attributable, as well, to the smaller audience for literary works, even the kinds that, as shown in this study, have broken the sound barrier between popular and academic sales. In constructing Canadian fame in this manner, Canada's Walk of Fame replicates the very situation that I identified at the beginning of this book: the feeling that literary celebrity is itself a contradiction in terms. In this respect, it is meaningful that when Atwood received her star on the Canadian Walk of Fame, she was photographed alongside Joni Mitchell, two women joking as they bent to point at their newly minted stars. This was the photograph that the *Globe and Mail* chose to run to illustrate its coverage of the event, and its caption read 'Concrete evidence of fame.' The presence of a star in the recording industry confirms the celebrity of the writer, just as the global appeal of a Canadian celebrity cements (in this case, literally) her fame at home.

This downplaying of literary celebrity might make Canada's Walk of Fame seem an odd choice as a concluding paradigm for this book, but I began this study by noting the reasons why literary celebrity, at first a seeming oxymoron to many, matters, why it should not pale in comparison with its more hyped celluloid variety. Canada's Walk of Fame embodies many of the tensions and complexities surrounding Canadian celebrity in general, including this tendency to sideline the literary in favour of more popular entertainment. But what particularly interests me about the Walk of Fame, as an analogue to the phenomenon of literary celebrity that I have studied here, is its unconscious conflictedness about discourses of celebrity and citizenship.

To begin with, the model for any such walk derives from American culture, specifically from the Hollywood Walk of Fame that is located on the streets that converge on Hollywood Boulevard, but the relation between our two walks is conflicted, to say the least. Founders of Canada's Walk of Fame define their project in terms that explicitly distinguish it from the Holly-

wood version, even as they clearly imitate that model. In a number of online volunteer-authored encyclopedias, like Wikipedia
and answersnow.com, the exact same text appears as the entry
for 'Canada's Walk of Fame,' so I suspect that this text was probably authored by the Walk's publicity people or, at the very least,
by an enthusiast. The first section of this entry deals with how
our Walk of Fame differs from Hollywood's, clearly a point of
some anxiety that organizers wish to clear up right away, particularly since the Walk was criticized in the press in its first few
years of operation as an ersatz Hollywood knock-off.

Of those national differences that Canada's Walk of Fame
promoters so wish to emphasize, the one I find most revealing is
the economic one. The Wikipedia entry rightly notes that the
Hollywood Walk of Fame requires that stars (or, more typically,
their movie studios, record companies, or management) pay an
'upkeep fee.' But on the Hollywood Walk of Fame's Web site,
that fee, a substantial US$15,000, is called a 'sponsorship fee,'
and it is not only for upkeep of the star but to cover additional
costs such as personal security for the star during the dedication
ceremony. Indeed, Canada's Walk of Fame chair Peter Soumalias commented in an interview that personal security is a major
source of differences of opinion between American and Canadian handlings of these sorts of ceremonies; as he observed,
'The publicists and managers for Canadian celebrities based in
Los Angeles often want to be sure that there are private and
secure areas for their clients at the event, so they don't have to
mix and mingle with everyday people. However, it's been our
experience that the stars want to mix with people once they get
here' ('Canada's Walk of Fame,' BizBash). There are, I would
argue, both real and perceived cultural differences at work
here. Certainly, American publicists' concerns mirror the fears
about a discernable gun culture; the disparity in handgun ownership between the United States and Canada cannot be
denied. But at the same time, the clichéd figure of the down-to-
earth Canuck who is unaffected by fame is on view here.

If a monetary fee ensures this American segregation of celebrities from the anonymous crowd, then Canada's Walk of Fame

would logically be eager to define itself, correspondingly, as a non-profit organization. This is exactly what the publicity entry for the Walk does. The 'Canadian counterpart' to Hollywood's Walk of Fame, it tells us, 'actually is a true hall of fame' because it does not charge a fee; these celebrities 'thus must earn their honour' ('Canada's Walk of Fame' *Wikipedia*). Here the promoters of the Walk explicitly touch on one of the sensitive points of celebrity culture that I have referred to at several points in this study: the troubled relation between fame and the labour that would earn, and therefore justify, that fame. Canadians are positioned as honest labourers whose fame is to be distinguished from a less labour-reliant form of American celebrity.

By denying economic factors in its selection process, therefore, Canada's Walk of Fame organizers claim its authenticity as a star-confirming mechanism. As Soumalias declares, Canadian inductees 'understand that it is a tribute and not a marketing scheme' (Dios 14). Even the term chosen by Soumalias, 'tribute' signals a pretension to a Bourdeusian cultural capital that is meant to outclass the crassness of a mere 'marketing scheme.' But this idealistic rhetoric obscures the fact that the Walk is, and has been from its inception, an economic undertaking. For the first few years of its operations, the Walk depended on government grants for more than half of its operating budget, but by 2003 it was funded entirely through private sources. Asked about this, Soumalias explained that the board made this decision because, as he put it, 'Governments come and go, policies change, and you don't want to be susceptible to the whims of a new administration' ('Canada's Walk of Fame,' BizBash). However, the very instability of governments arguably brought Canada's Walk of Fame into being in the first place. Soumalias was co-chair of former Toronto mayor Mel Lastman's successful campaign for that office in 1998. The Walk went into operation that same year, substantially helped along by Lastman's support.

As years went on, other corporate partners came on board, making the eventual transition to private funding in 2003, the year that David Miller succeeded Lastman as mayor. The Walk's current Web site, in comparison with its earlier incarnations, is a veritable patchwork of corporate logos. Sponsors include MasterCard, Volkswagen, Air Canada, Chanel, and NBC-Universal. Like literary celebrity itself, as Bourdieu would argue, the language of cultural capital and achievement is built upon an unacknowledged substratum of economic capital. The problem, however, isn't simply the fact that the Walk has corporate backing; my aim, instead, is to complicate the Walk's claims of economic disinterestedness, particularly as that discourse is harnessed in the interests of constructing a distinctly Canadian approach to fame.

On one hand, Canada's Walk of Fame's proceedings and publicity materials explicitly mobilize a by-now familiar discourse of Canadian nationalism; their Web site's photo gallery of red carpet ceremonies features several of these stars posing with a row of smiling, red-clad Mounties. However, in its 2004 selections, the Walk of Fame's board made its cross-border connections explicit; three of the nine inductees that year were honoured in the category 'Hollywood Pioneers': film magnates Louis B. Mayer, Mack Sennett, and Jack Warner. In terms of selection criteria, the Walk negotiates some of the tricky border-crossing issues that faced Carol Shields; nominees must either be born in Canada or spend their 'formative or creative years in Canada' (Canada's Walk of Fame/Allée des celebrités). Thus, just by virtue of their Canadian birthplaces, these mainly American-identified captains of Hollywood industry qualify to be recognized as Canadian celebrities. The Hollywood Walk of Fame, on the other hand, has no such citizenship requirement.

Such ironies have not been lost on some critics of the Walk; as Lynn Crosbie wrote in the *Globe and Mail*, 'There is a good reason that Canada has never had this kind of monument [i.e., the Hollywood Walk of Fame], as the history of Canadian talent – particularly in the arts and entertainment field – is an expatriate history' (R6). Clearly, this is an overstatement, as even a cursory glance at the slate of 101 inductees to date will show. But Crosbie's statement contains within it a measure of truth, as the presence of Monty Hall, Michael J. Fox, or Jim Carrey –

who, Crosbie notes, was renouncing his Canadian citizenship at his time of induction – suggests. Such inductees sit oddly, to be sure, with the bizarre RCMP Musical Ride vibe of the ceremonies.

Crosbie's critique of this construction of Canadian fame resonates with recent developments in the study of Canadian literature – specifically, the recent publication of Nick Mount's study *When Canadian Literature Moved to New York*. There, Mount provocatively argues that 'Canadian literature began here [in New York] ... not in the backwoods of Ontario, not on the salt flats of New Brunswick, but in the cafés, publishing offices, and boarding houses of late nineteenth-century New York' (18). Many of Mount's claims will be questioned, and ensuing debate will be productive, but what is germane to my present study is the persistence of the debate itself: Mount's questioning of what, exactly, is Canadian about the Canadian literary canon is echoed in national institutions like Canada's Walk of Fame that seek both to promote nationalism and to acknowledge the global outreach of Canadian celebrity as a means of justifying that celebrity, of making it 'qualify.' Similarly, Mount decries what he sees as the efforts of the next generation of Canadian writers and literary critics to expunge the contributions of émigré authors in the interests of narrating a determinedly Canadian literary history because he feels that these expatriates are an important part of our national literary narrative, but he also makes strong claims for them as continentalists, products of globalization *avant la lettre*. As Mount says in closing his book, 'Canadian writers have been *practising* transnationalism since before there was a Canadian literature' (162). So his own critical situating of expatriate writers shifts between a reformulated nationalism and a celebration of proto-postnationalism.

The official logo for Canada's Walk of Fame evinces the same uneasy cross-pollination of nationalisms and global culture. Though Andrew Flynn reported that, 'unlike the original sidewalk squares in Hollywood, the Walk of Fame plaques display not a star but a stylized maple leaf and signature of the celebrity' (Flynn), this is not quite accurate. If one looks closely at that maple leaf, either on the Walk of Fame's Web site or, especially, on the plaques themselves, one can see that this stylized maple leaf is, in fact, star-shaped. It is, in effect, a Canadian maple leaf morphing into a star. In its very shape, therefore, the Canadian Walk of Fame logo dramatizes the process of celebrity as a movement from the local to the global; this morphed leaf-star seems, in fact, almost admonitory in its collectivism. It appears to warn its special individual recipients that, however brightly they shine in the global firmament of celebrity, they must remain Canucks at heart.

What does all of this mean for literary celebrity in Canada? What happens to writers when they 'walk the walk' that is celebrity? What I conclude is that Canadian literary celebrity, like all forms of celebrity, is crucially caught up in determinations and negotiations about citizenship. There is an ongoing competition, as I have noted, between local and global ownership of celebrity; just as theorists such as P. David Marshall or Richard Dyer have generally seen celebrity as a proving ground for performances of subjectivities, I think that it is the subject as citizen that is crucially at issue in celebrity. The uneasiness and tensions that I have explored in studying the public faces of Atwood, Shields, Ondaatje, and their predecessors, Montgomery, Leacock, Johnson, and de la Roche, grow out of, among other things, conflicting and competing ideas about what sort of citizen celebrity makes of the subject. This citizenship might have any number of dimensions or placements: politically active Mohawk or commodified Indian princess in the case of Pauline Johnson; adopted mainstream Canadian or exoticized and eroticized other, in the case of Michael Ondaatje, to name but two examples.

What is also crucially at stake for Canadian writers involved in the game of fame is the uneasy dance that so many of them do – and, historically, have done – between economic success and cultural respect. The fabled high culture versus pop culture divide that has fuelled so much discussion over the decades does not appear to be such a decided clash from the point of view of literary celebrity in Canada. The writers I have studied each radically question, in one way or another, any such easy division between pleasing a larger audience and gaining literary respect, however much any of those writers have agonized over losing cultural capital in the process of supporting themselves as writers. The term 'middlebrow' comes closest to capturing this refusal of the ends of the cultural production spectrum, and yet this study suggests to me that what is happening is a constant, nervous juggling of the two forms of capital rather than the formation of a stable in-between category of literary value.

Finally, in questioning the adequacy of such polarized labels, I hope that the present study adds to the growing tendency to avoid, or at least to try to avoid, automatically negative assumptions about celebrity and its workings. In this analysis, I have steered away from gloomy prognostications about increasing commercialization and from nostalgic yearnings for a golden age when writers were valued for their achievements alone. As Pauline Johnson, Stephen Leacock, Mazo de la Roche, L.M. Montgomery, Margaret Atwood, Michael Ondaatje, and Carol Shields have helped me to show, things were never quite that simple. Celebrity has had its benefits as well as its pitfalls for writers, and rather than unproblematically hailing the celebrity of writers as national heroes or seeing the evidence of celebrity or popularity as lowering the value of a writer's work, we need to acknowledge frankly the workings of celebrity in all cultural venues.

In a *New Yorker* cartoon of a few years ago, an author is shown speaking on the telephone to his agent, wild-eyed and excited. He says into the telephone, 'Mud wrestle in my underwear on national TV while holding up a copy of my new book? NO PROBLEMO!' The caption under the comic reads 'Thomas Pynchon's evil twin.' A reconceptualization of literary celebrity along the lines I am suggesting, as being more about conflicting allegiances to forms of citizenship and capital, may prevent us from redrawing these boundaries between highbrow and popular art, between publicity and privacy, quite so easily. Rather than seeing celebrity as the Hyde to every serious writer's Jekyll, it is just one of the many ways in which writers – and all of us, as both performers and consumers of celebrity at various cultural sites – negotiate the local, national, and global spaces in which we find ourselves.

Works Cited

Adams, James. 'Shields's Talents Gained World Acclaim.' *Globe and Mail* 18 July 2003: A1, A6.

Adams, Tim. Rev. of *Anil's Ghost*, by Michael Ondaatje. 13 March 2002. Mail and Guardian online http://www.mg.co.za/mg/books/0006/000620–anilsghost.html. Accessed 12 May 2002.

Akamatsu, Yoshiko. 'Japanese Readings of *Anne of Green Gables*.' Gammel and Epperly 201–12.

Andrews, Marke. 'Pulitzer Prize Hasn't Changed Carol Shields' Life, She Says.' *Vancouver Sun* 20 Oct. 1995: C1, C7.

'Appendix to a Preliminary Study of the Stephen Leacock Memorial Home and the Feasibility of Long-Term Development.' Janus Museum Consultants Ltd. Toronto. July 1967.

Atwood, Margaret. *Alias Grace*. Toronto: McClelland and Stewart, 1996.

– *Cat's Eye*. 1988. Toronto: Seal, 1999.

– 'If You Can't Say Something Nice, Don't Say Anything at All.' *Language in Her Eye: Writing and Gender: Views by Canadian Women Writing in English*. Ed. Libby Scheier, Sarah Sheard, and Eleanor Wachtel. Toronto: Coach House, 1990. 15–25.

– *Lady Oracle*. 1976. Toronto: McClelland-Bantam, 1977.

– *Negotiating with the Dead: A Writer on Writing*. Cambridge: Cambridge UP, 2002.

– 'Revisiting Anne.' Gammel and Epperly 222–6.

'Atwood's Booker Win.' Australian Broadcast Company online. http://www.abc.net.au/worldtoday/s209839.htm. Accessed 12 June 2002.

Ayre, John. 'How a Gothic Girl Became Canada's Top Literary Star.' *Globe and Mail* 29 Aug. 1998: D14.

Becker, Susanne. 'Celebrity, or a Disneyland of the Soul: Margaret Atwood and the Media.' Nischik 28–40.

Besner, Neil K., ed. *Carol Shields: The Arts of a Writing Life.* Winnipeg: Prairie Fire P, 2003.

Boorstin, Daniel. *The Image: Or What Happened to the American Dream.* New York: Atheneum, 1962.

Bourdieu, Pierre. *The Field of Cultural Production: Essays on Art and Literature.* Ed. and introd. Randal Johnson. New York: Columbia UP, 1993.

Bratton, Daniel L. *Thirty-Two Short Views of Mazo de la Roche.* Toronto: ECW P, 1996.

Brennan, Timothy. *At Home in the World: Cosmopolitanism Now.* Cambridge: Harvard UP, 1997.

– 'Cosmopolitans and Celebrities.' *Race and Class* 31.1 (1989): 1–20.

Bush, Catherine. 'Michael Ondaatje: An Interview.' *Essays on Canadian Writing* 53 (1994): 238–49.

Buss, Helen. 'Abducting Mary and Carol: Reading Carol Shields's *Swann* and the Representation of the Writer through Theories of Biographical Recognition.' *English Studies in Canada* 23.4 (1997): 427–41.

Butterfield, Martha. 'The One Lighted Room: *In the Skin of a Lion.*' *Canadian Literature* 119 (1988): 162–7.

Cameron, Donald. *Faces of Leacock.* Toronto: Ryerson, 1967.

– 'Stephen Leacock: The Boy behind the Arras.' *Journal of Commonwealth Literature* 3 (1967): 3–18.

Canada's Walk of Fame. http://www.canadaswalkoffame.com. Accessed 25 May 2006.

'Canada's Walk of Fame.' BizBash.TO. http://www.bizbash.com/toronto/content/editorial/e5981.asp. Accessed 23 May 2006.

'Canada's Walk of Fame.' *Wikipedia.* http://en.wikipedia.org/wiki/Canada's_Walk_of_Fame. Accessed 23 May 2006.

Canada's Walk of Fame / Allée des celebrités Canadiennes. http://www.canadaswalkoffame.com. Accessed 23 May 2006.

CBC. Life and Times. http://www.tv.cbc.ca/lifeandtimes/bio1999/
leacock.htm. Accessed 28 Jan. 2002.

CBC. National Magazine. http://cbc.news/national/magazine/
atwood/. Accessed 12 June 2002.

'Celebrate Canada Book Day with Stephen Leacock!' Literary Partners
of Manitoba. http://www.mb.literacy.ca/whatnew/leacock
.leacock.htm. Accessed 20 Jan. 2003.

Cherney, Elena, and Donna Bailey Nurse. 'Booklover Oprah Gets
Literary Prize.' *National Post* 18 Nov. 1999: A3.

Collison, Robert. 'Margaret Atwood Takes N.Y.C.' *Chatelaine* June 1986:
64–5+.

Colombo, John Robert. *Canadian Literary Landmarks.* Willowdale, ON:
Hounslow, 1984.

Conlogue, Ray. 'Canada's Gentle "Literary Lioness".' *Globe and Mail* 8
April 2002: R3.

Cooke, Nathalie. 'Lions, Tigers, and Pussycats: Margaret Atwood
(Auto-) Biographically.' Nischik 15–27.

Crabb, Michael. 'Winnipeg Launches "Carol Shields' Book Award."'
CBC Infoculture, 23 April 1999. www.infoculture.cbc.ca. Accessed 12
Jan. 2001.

Crosbie, Lynn. 'The Hawk Makes the Walk.' *Globe and Mail* 5 Oct. 2002:
R6.

Curry Ralph. 'Introduction.' *Christmas with Stephen Leacock: Reflections on
the Yuletide Season.* Toronto: National Heritage Books, 1988. 9–11.

Curry, Ralph. 'Leacock and the Media.' Staines 23–31.

Davey, Frank. *Canadian Literary Power.* The Writer as Critic Series 4.
Edmonton: NeWest, 1994.

Daymond, D.M. 'Mazo de la Roche.' *Canadian Writers, 1920–1959.* Dic-
tionary of Literary Biography 68. Ed. W.H New. Detroit: Gale, 1988.
106–12.

deCordova, Richard. 'The Emergence of the Star System in America.'
Gledhill 17–29.

– *Picture Personalities: The Emergence of the Star System in America.* Urbana:
U of Illinois P, 1990.

de la Roche, Mazo. *Ringing the Changes: An Autobiography.* Boston: Little, Brown, 1957.

Dios, Wolfgang. 'The Long Walk Home: The Road to Canada's Walk of Fame.' *Marquee* 26.5 (2001): 14.

Doyle, James. *Stephen Leacock: The Sage of Orillia.* Toronto: ECW P, 1992.

Duffy, Dennis. 'Mazo de la Roche.' *Oxford Companion to Canadian Literature.* 2nd ed. Ed. William Toye. Toronto: Oxford UP, 1997. 103–4.

Dyer, Richard. '*A Star Is Born* and the Construction of Authenticity.' Gledhill 132–40.

– *Stars.* 1979. 2nd ed. London: British Film Institute, 1998.

Eagleton, Mary. 'Carol Shields and Pierre Bourdieu: Reading *Swann.*' *Critique* 44.3 (2003): 313–28.

Eden, Edward, and Dee Goertz, eds. *Carol Shields, Narrative Hunger, and the Possibilities of Fiction.* Toronto: U of Toronto P, 2003.

Ellis, John. *Visible Fictions: Cinema: Television: Video.* London: Routledge, 1992.

Ellmann, Richard. *Oscar Wilde.* 1984. New York: Vintage, 1988.

Epperly, Elizabeth R. 'Approaching the Montgomery Manuscripts.' *Harvesting Thistles: The Textual Garden of L.M. Montgomery.* Ed. Mary Henley Rubio. Guelph, ON: Canadian Children's Press, 1994. 74–83.

– 'L.M. Montgomery and the Changing Times.' *Acadiensis* 17.2 (1998): 177–85.

Fiamengo, Janice. 'Reconsidering Pauline.' *Canadian Literature* 167 (2000): 174–6.

Finkle, Derek. 'A Vow of Silence.' *Saturday Night* Nov. 1996: 90–4, 96+.

Flynn, Andrew. 'Joni Mitchell, Margaret Atwood Added to Stars on Walk of Fame.' Canadian Press Newswire. 19 Oct. 2001.

Forbes, Leslie. 'More Spice Than Nice.' *Globe and Mail* 26 Feb. 2000: D2–D3.

Francis, Daniel. *The Imaginary Indian: The Image of the Indian in Canadian Culture.* Vancouver: Arsenal Pulp, 1992.

Freedman, Adele. 'Happy Heroine and "Freak" of CanLit.' *Globe and Mail* 25 Oct. 1980: E1.

Freeman, Alan. 'Belle of the Booker.' *Globe and Mail* 9 Nov. 2000: R1, R7.

French, William. 'Icon and Target: Atwood as Thing.' *Globe and Mail* 7 April 1973: 28.

– 'I'm an Expert on Anorexia.' *Globe and Mail* 3 Nov. 1983: E1.

Fulford, Robert. 'Do Canadians Fear Excellence? Consider the Case of Atwood.' *Saturday Night* May 1980: 12.

Gabler, Neal. *Life, the Movie: How Entertainment Conquered Reality.* New York: Vintage, 1998.

Gaines, Jane M. *Contested Culture: The Image, the Voice, and the Law.* Chapel Hill: U of North Carolina P, 1991.

Gammel, Irene, and Elizabeth Epperly. Introduction. 'L.M. Montgomery and the Shaping of Canadian Culture.' Gammel and Epperly 3–13.

– eds. *L.M. Montgomery and Canadian Culture.* Toronto: U of Toronto P, 1999.

Gamson, Joshua. *Claims to Fame: Celebrity in Contemporary America.* Berkeley: U of California P, 1994.

Gefen, Pearl Sheffy. 'If I Were 19 Now, I'd Maybe Want to Be a Filmmaker.' *Globe and Mail* 4 May 1990: D3.

Gerson, Carole. 'Dragged at Anne's Chariot Wheels: L.M. Montgomery and the Sequels to *Anne of Green Gables*.' *Part Two: Reflections on the Sequel.* Ed. Paul Budra and Betty Schellenberg. Toronto: U of Toronto P, 1998. 144–59.

– 'The Most Canadian of All Canadian Poets: Pauline Johnson and the Construction of a National Literature.' *Canadian Literature* 158 (1998): 90–107.

– *A Purer Taste: The Writing and Reading of Fiction in English in Nineteenth-Century Canada.* Toronto: U of Toronto P, 1989.

Gerstel, Judy. 'Doctoring the Patient.' *Toronto Star* 8 Nov. 1996: D1, D4.

Gillen, Mollie. *The Wheel of Things: A Biography of L.M. Montgomery.* Don Mills, ON: Fitzhenry & Whiteside, 1975.

Givner, Joan. 'Deciphering the Female Self: Writing the Life of Mazo de la Roche: Proposal for a Series of Three Programs on CBC Radio's "Ideas."' *Room of One's Own* 15.3–4 (1992): 194–209.

– *Mazo de la Roche: The Hidden Life.* Toronto: Oxford UP, 1989.

Glass, Loren. *Authors Inc.: Literary Celebrity in the Modern United States, 1880–1980.* New York: New York UP, 2004.

Gledhill, Christine, ed. *Stardom: Industry of Desire.* London: Routledge, 1991.

Goodman, Lee-Anne. 'Ondaatje Guards Privacy in Face of Worldwide Interest.' *Canadian Press Newswire* 25 March 1997.

Hambleton, Ronald. *Mazo de la Roche of Jalna*. New York: Hawthorn, 1966.

– *The Secret of Jalna*. Don Mills, ON: PaperJacks, 1972.

Hamilton, Ian. *Robert Lowell: A Biography*. New York: Random House, 1982.

Hammill, Faye. 'The Sensations of the 1920s: Martha Ostenso's *Wild Geese* and Mazo de la Roche's *Jalna*.' *Studies in Canadian Literature* 28.2 (2003): 74–97.

Hancock, Geoff. 'This Little Peggy Went to Market: Atwood on Being an International Literary Success.' *Books in Canada* June-July 1980: 30–1.

Heer, Jeet. 'Literary Gathering Intended to Be a Celebration of Carol Shields.' *National Post* 5 April 2002: B6.

Heilbron, Alexandra. *Remembering Lucy Maud Montgomery*. Toronto: Dundurn, 2001.

Hill, Maude Pettit. 'The Best Known Woman in Prince Edward Island: L.M. Montgomery Author of *Anne of Green Gables*.' *Chatelaine: A Magazine for Canadian Women* May 1928: 8–9, 65; June 1928: 23, 41.

Hollenberg, Donna Krolik. 'An Interview with Carol Shields.' *Contemporary Literature* 39.3 (1998): 339–55.

Honoré, Carl. 'The Enormous Pleasure of Making Something.' *National Post* 31 Jan. 2000: D12.

Horton, Jerry. 'Big Numbers, Low Profile.' *Quill and Quire* Jan. 1995: 14.

Houpt, Simon. 'Our Pick of Canada's Best: Showered with the Kind of Acclaim for His Latest Novel that Most Writers Only Dream of, Michael Ondaatje Remains Modest and Self-Effacing.' *Globe and Mail* 28 Dec. 2000. R1–R2.

Huggan, Graham. 'Exoticism and Ethnicity in Michael Ondaatje's *Running in the Family*.' *Essays on Canadian Writing* 57 (1995): 116–27.

– *The Postcolonial Exotic: Marketing the Margins*. London: Routledge, 2001.

Hughes, Lesley. 'The Shields Diaries.' *Chatelaine* April 1996: 110+.

Hunter, Lynette. *Outsider Notes: Feminist Approaches to Nation, State, Ideology, Writers/Readers and Publishing*. Vancouver: Talonbooks, 1996.

Italie, Hillel. 'Coming through Success.' *Vancouver Sun* 6 July 1999: C4, C6.

Jaffe, Aaron. *Modernism and the Culture of Celebrity.* Cambridge: Cambridge UP, 2005.

Johnson, Brian D. 'Maclean's Honour Roll 2000: Michael Ondaatje.' *Maclean's* 18 Dec. 2000: 67.

Johnston, Sheila M.F. *Buckskin and Broadcloth: A Celebration of E. Pauline Johnson Tekahionwake, 1861–1913.* Toronto: Natural Heritage, 1997.

Jones, Frank. 'Atwood Hits the Big Time.' *Toronto Star* 9 March 1980: D1.

Karr, Clarence. *Authors and Audiences: Popular Canadian Fiction in the Early Twentieth Century.* Toronto: McGill-Queen's UP, 2000.

Keller, Betty. *Pauline: A Biography of Pauline Johnson.* Vancouver: Douglas & McIntyre, 1981.

– *Pauline Johnson: First Aboriginal Voice of Canada.* Lantzville, BC: XYZ Publishing, 1999.

Kimball, Elizabeth. *The Man in the Panama Hat: Reminiscences of My Uncle, Stephen Leacock.* Toronto: McClelland and Stewart, 1970.

Kirk, Heather. 'Heritage under Siege: Leacock's Legacy Lives On, but the Places Associated with Him Are Definitely at Risk.' *Books in Canada* 21.8 (1992): 22–6.

Koring, Paul. 'Ondaatje Shares Booker Prize.' *Globe and Mail* 14 Oct. 1992: A1–A2.

Lacey, Liam. 'Michael Ondaatje: In the Skin of the Filmmaker.' *Globe and Mail* 9 Nov. 1996: C4.

Lamey, Andy. 'Ondaatje's New Novel Missing at Chapters.' *National Post* 25 March 2000: A2.

Lecker, Robert, ed. *Canadian Canons: Essays in Literary Value.* Toronto: U of Toronto P, 1991.

– *Making It Real: The Canonization of English-Canadian Literature.* Toronto: Anansi, 1995.

Legate, David M. *Stephen Leacock: A Biography.* Toronto: Doubleday, 1970.

Leighton, Mary Elizabeth. 'Performing Pauline Johnson: Representations of "The Indian Poetess" in the Periodical Press.' *Essays on Canadian Writing* 65 (1998): 141–64.

Livesay, Dorothy. 'Remembering Mazo.' *Selected Stories of Mazo de la Roche.* Ed. Douglas Daymond. Ottawa: U of Ottawa P, 1979. 11–13.

Lucas, Alec. 'The Achievement of Stephen Leacock.' Staines 121–5.

Lynes, Jeanette. 'Consumable Avonlea: The Commodification of the Green Gables Mythology.' *Canadian Children's Literature* 91–2 (1998): 7–21.

Lyon, George W. 'Pauline Johnson: A Reconsideration.' *Studies in Canadian Literature / Etudes en Littérature Canadienne* 15:2 (1990): 136–59.

Lyons, John. 'A Lucky Life.' *Winnipeg Free Press* 17 Oct. 1993: 3–4.

– 'Shields Takes Nomination in Stride.' *Winnipeg Free Press* 25 Sept. 1993: B3.

MacGregor, Roy. 'Atwood's World.' *Maclean's* 15 Oct. 1979: 64–6.

Mallick, Heather. 'The World Is Not Nice, and Margaret Atwood Knows It.' *Globe and Mail* 18 Nov. 2000: E3.

Marchand, Philip. 'Aggressively Silent Michael Ondaatje.' *Toronto Star* 19 Sept. 1992: G1, G10.

Margaret Atwood Official Website. http://www.owtoad.com. Accessed 12 June 2002.

Margolis, Stacey. 'The Public Life: The Discourse of Privacy in the Age of Celebrity.' *Arizona Quarterly* 51.2 (1995): 81–101.

Marshall, P. David. *Celebrity and Power: Fame in Contemporary Culture.* Minneapolis: U of Minnesota P, 1997.

Martin, Sandra. 'After the Party.' *Globe and Mail* 15 Jan. 2001. R1, R5.

– 'Giller Prize Drama Ends in a Tie.' *Globe and Mail* 3 Nov. 2000: A20.

McCracken, Grant. 'Who Is the Celebrity Endorser? Cultural Foundations of the Endorsement Process.' *Journal of Consumer Research* 16.3 (1989): 310–21.

Mills, C. Wright. *The Power Elite.* New York: Oxford UP, 1956.

Moir, Jan. 'Shields Masters Culture Clash.' *Calgary Herald* 29 Jan. 2000: ES2.

Monaco, James, ed. *Celebrity: The Media as Image Makers.* New York: Delta, 1978.

Montgomery, L.M. *The Alpine Path: The Story of My Career.* 1917. Don Mills, ON: Fitzhenry & Whiteside, 1975.

– *The Green Gables Letters: From L.M. Montgomery to Ephraim Weber, 1905–1909.* Ed. Wilfrid Eggleston. 1960. Ottawa: Borealis, 1981.

– 'L.M. Montgomery's Ideas: As Submitted to the Editor of a Toronto Newspaper by L.M. Montgomery in Response to a Critical Review of *Magic for Marigold* in 1930.' *Kindred Spirits* Autumn 1996: 9–10.

- *My Dear Mr. M.: Letters to G.B. MacMillan from L.M. Montgomery.* Ed. Francis W.P. Bolger and Elizabeth R. Epperly. 1980. Toronto: Oxford UP, 1992.
- 'Red Scrapbook #1.' L.M. Montgomery Collection, U of Guelph archives.
- 'Red Scrapbook #2.' L.M. Montgomery Collection, U of Guelph archives.
- 'Scrapbook of Book Reviews.' L.M. Montgomery Collection, U of Guelph Archives.
- *The Selected Journals of L.M. Montgomery.* Volume 1. 1889–1910. Ed. Mary Rubio and Elizabeth Waterston. Toronto: Oxford UP, 1985.
- *The Selected Journals of L.M. Montgomery.* Volume 3. *1921–1929.* Ed. Mary Rubio and Elizabeth Waterston. Toronto: Oxford UP, 1992.
- *The Selected Journals of L.M. Montgomery.* Volume 4. *1929–1935.* Ed. Mary Rubio and Elizabeth Waterston. Toronto: Oxford UP, 1998.
Moran, Joe. *Star Authors: Literary Celebrity in America.* London: Pluto, 2000.
Morin, Edgar. *The Stars.* Evergreen Profile Book 7. Trans. Richard Howard. New York: Grove, 1960.
Moritz, Albert, and Theresa Moritz. *Leacock: A Biography.* Toronto: Stoddart, 1985.
Mount, Nick. *When Canadian Literature Moved to New York.* Toronto: U of Toronto P, 2005.
Mukherjee, Arun. *Oppositional Aesthetics: Readings from a Hyphenated Space.* Toronto: TSAR, 1994.
Neville, William. 'Carol Shields and Winnipeg: Finding Home.' Besner 27–37.
'News from the L.M. Montgomery Institute.' *Kindred Spirits* Summer 1997: 24.
Nickson, Keith. 'The Ondaatje Mystique.' *Books in Canada* Dec. 1992. 6–7.
Nischik, Reingard M., ed. *Margaret Atwood: Works and Impact.* Rochester, NY: Camden House, 2000.
Ondaatje, Michael. *Anil's Ghost.* Toronto: McClelland and Stewart, 2000.
- *The Cinnamon Peeler: Selected Poems.* 1989. Toronto: McClelland and Stewart, 1994.

– *The Collected Works of Billy the Kid: Left-Handed Poems.* 1970. Toronto: Anansi, 1997.
– *Coming Through Slaughter.* 1976. Toronto: Vintage Canada, 1998.
– *The Conversations: Walter Murch and the Art of Editing Film.* Toronto: Vintage Canada, 2002.
– *The English Patient.* 1992. Toronto: Vintage, 1993.
– *Handwriting.* Toronto: McClelland and Stewart, 1998.
– *In the Skin of a Lion.* 1987. Toronto: Vintage, 1996.
– *Running in the Family.* 1982. Toronto: McClelland and Stewart, 1993.
Ondaatje, Michael, and Atom Egoyan. 'The Kitchen Table Talks.' *Globe and Mail* 8 April 2000: D6–D7.
Owens, Anne-Marie. 'Am-Lit's Appropriation of Atwood.' *National Post* 13 Jan. 2001: B1, B6.
Panofsky, Ruth. 'At Odds: Reviewers and Readers of the Jalna Novels.' *Studies in Canadian Literature* 25.1 (2000): 57–72.
– '"Don't Let Me Do It!": Mazo de la Roche and Her Publishers.' *International Journal of Canadian Studies / Revue internationale d'études canadiennes* 11 (1995): 171–84.
Parks Canada. Stephen Leacock Museum Website. http://parkscan-ada.pch.gc.ca/nhs/nonadmin/english/museum_e.htm. Accessed 28 January 2002.
Pearce, Jon. *Twelve Voices: Interviews with Canadian Poets.* Ottawa: Borealis, 1980.
Pike, E. Holly 'Mass Marketing, Popular Culture, and the Canadian Celebrity Author.' *Making Avonlea: L.M. Montgomery and Popular Culture.* Ed. Irene Gammel. Toronto: U of Toronto P, 2002. 238–51.
Postman, Neil. *Amusing Ourselves to Death: Public Discourse in the Age of Show Business.* New York: Viking Penguin, 1985.
Power, Carla. 'Jazz in Strange Places: *The English Patient*'s Author Is the Movie's Biggest Fan.' *Newsweek* 24 March 1997: 82.
Prokosh, Kevin. 'Spotlight Bothersome for Novelist.' *Winnipeg Free Press* 18 Sept. 1993: B3.
Prokosh, Kevin, and Linda Rosborough. 'Shields Belongs to History.' *Winnipeg Free Press* 19 April 1995: C8.

Quattrin, Linda. '"You Get Braver": Novelist, Poet, Prof and Mom Carol Shields "Just Drifted Along" to Success.' *Winnipeg Free Press* 29 Feb. 1992: C25.

Rasporich, Beverly J. 'The Leacock Persona and the Canadian Character.' *Mosaic* 14:2 (1981): 77–92.

Ratliff, Ben. 'Ondaatje Learns to Deal with the Fame Bestowed by Oscar.' *Vancouver Sun* 29 March 1997: G1, G4.

Ray, Nina M. 'The Endorsement Potential Also Rises: The Merchandising of Ernest Hemingway.' *Hemingway Review* 13.2 (1994): 74–86.

Renzetti, Elizabeth. 'Convention Becomes Carol Shields.' *Globe and Mail* 18 Sept. 1997: D7.

Ricci, Nino. 'A Tribute to Carol Shields.' *Brick* 69 (2002): 170–5.

Richler, Noah. 'We Will Be Made to Atone for This.' *National Post* 8 Nov. 2000: B1, B4.

Ridley, Hilda M. *The Story of L.M. Montgomery.* London: Harrap, 1956.

Righton, Barbara. 'People.' *Maclean's* 4 Oct. 1982: 36.

Ringer, Janet. 'Acclaimed Writer Carol Shields Leaving Winnipeg.' CBC Infoculture, 20 July 1999. www.infoculture.cbc.ca. Accessed 12 Jan. 2001.

Rojek, Chris. *Celebrity.* London: Reaktion, 2001.

Rootland, Nancy. *Anne's World, Maud's World: The Sacred Sites of L.M. Montgomery.* Halifax: Nimbus, 1996.

Rosborough, Linda. 'Award Expected to Spur Sales.' *Winnipeg Free Press* 1 March 1995: D8.

– 'She's One of Ours: Awards Gala Embraces Shields.' *Winnipeg Free Press* 23 April 1995: D6.

Rosenthal, Caroline. 'Canonizing Atwood: Her Impact on Teaching in the U.S., Canada, and Europe.' Nischik 41–56.

Ross, Cecily. 'Fame's Breath Hot on Ondaatje.' *Financial Post* 26–8 Sept. 1992: S16.

Ross, Val. 'Atwood Industry Goes Global.' *Globe and Mail* 7 Sept. 1996: A1, A6.

– 'Battle of Avonlea Being Waged by Beloved Author's Heirs.' *Globe and Mail* 7 July 1999: E1.

– 'Minefields of the Mind: Face to Face with Michael Ondaatje.' *Globe and Mail* 10 Oct. 1992: C1, C6.

- 'Playing the Atwood Guessing Game.' *Globe and Mail* 7 Oct. 1993: C1–C2.

Rubbo, Michael, dir. *Once in August.* Canadian Writers Series. National Film Board of Canada, 1984.

Rubio, Mary Henley. Introduction. 'Harvesting Thistles in Montgomery's Textual Garden.' *Harvesting Thistles: The Textual Garden of L.M. Montgomery. Essays on Her Novels and Journals.* Ed. Mary Henley Rubio. Guelph, ON: Canadian Children's P, 1994. 1–13.

Russo, Maria. 'Final Chapter.' *New York Times Magazine* 14 April 2002: 32–5.

Schickel, Richard. *Intimate Strangers: The Culture of Celebrity.* Garden City, NY: Doubleday, 1985.

Scobie, Stephen. '*Coming Through Slaughter:* Fictional Magnets and Spider's Webbs.' *Essays on Canadian Writing* 12 (1978): 5–23.

'Shields.' *Globe and Mail* 23 Oct. 1999: D4–D5.

Shields, Carol. *Swann.* 1987. Toronto: Vintage, 1996.

- *Unless: A Novel.* Toronto: Random House Canada, 2002.

Slinger, Helen. 'Interview with Margaret Atwood.' *Maclean's* 6 Sept. 1976: 6–7.

Solecki, Sam. 'Making and Destroying: Michael Ondaatje's *Coming through Slaughter* and Extremist Art.' *Essays on Canadian Writing* 12 (1978): 24–47.

Spicer, Nick. 'Atwood Joins Greats of English Literature.' *Sunday Herald* 15 Nov., 1998: D11.

Staines, David, ed. *Stephen Leacock: A Reappraisal.* Ottawa: U of Ottawa P, 1986.

Staton, Eleanor. 'Rejection Letters Are Nicer in Canada.' *Quill & Quire* January 1977: 18–19.

'Stephen Leacock' Links to Literature. http://www.linkstoliterature.com/leacock.htm. Accessed 28 Jan. 2002.

Stevenson, Melanie. 'Re-Staging Pauline Johnson.' Paper presented at the Association of Canadian College and University Teachers of English. Edmonton, May 2000.

Stoffman, Judy. 'Anne in Popular Japanese Culture.' *Canadian Children's Literature* 91–2 (1998): 53–63.

Strong-Boag, Veronica, and Carole Gerson. *Paddling Her Own Canoe:*

The Times and Texts of E. Pauline Johnson (Tekahionwake). Toronto: U of Toronto P, 2000.

'Such Darling Dodos.' Rev. of *Morning at Jalna* by Mazo de la Roche. *Times Literary Supplement* 29 July 1960: 477.

Thomas, Joan. '"Writing Must Come Out of What Passionately Interests Us. Nothing Else Will Do": An Epistolary Interview with Carol Shields.' *Prairie Fire* 16.1 (1995): 121–30.

Timson, Judith. 'The Magnificent Margaret Atwood.' *Chatelaine* Jan. 1981. 42+.

Toller, Carol. 'Oscar Spurs Sales of *The English Patient.*' *Quill and Quire* 63.5 (May 1997): 14.

'Toronto Woman Wins $10,000 Prize for Novel; 1,100 in *Atlantic Monthly*'s Competition.' *New York Times* 11 April 1927: 23.

Trillin, Calvin. 'Anne of Red Hair: What Do the Japanese See in *Anne of Green Gables?*' Gammel and Epperly 213–21.

Turbide, Diane. 'The Masculine Maze.' *Maclean's* 29 Sept. 1997: 82, 85.

– 'A Prairie Pulitzer.' *Maclean's* 1 May 1995: 76–7.

Turner, Graeme. *Understanding Celebrity.* London: Sage, 2004.

Twain, Mark. 'Hunting Celebrities.' *Independent* 53 (1901): 1357.

Tye, Diane. 'Multiple Meanings Called Cavendish: The Interaction of Tourism with Traditional Culture.' *Journal of Canadian Studies* 29 (1994): 122–34.

Unwin, Peter. 'Mohawk Princess: Few Poets Have Been More Beloved by Ordinary Canadians Than Pauline Johnson.' *Beaver* 79.5 (1999): 15–20.

Verhoeven, W.M. 'Playing Hide and Seek in Language: Michael Ondaatje's Historiography of the Self.' *American Review of Canadian Studies* 24.1 (1994): 21–38.

Viner, Katherine. 'Double Bluff.' Guardian online. http://books.guardian.co.uk/bookerprize2000/story/0,6194,377730,00.html. Accessed 12 June 2002.

Wachtel, Eleanor. 'Interview with Carol Shields.' *Room of One's Own* 13.1/2 (1989): 5–45.

– 'An Interview with Michael Ondaatje.' *Essays on Canadian Writing* 53 (1994): 250–61.

– 'Introduction.' *Room of One's Own*. The Carol Shields Issue. 13.1/2 (1989): 2–4.

Welsh-Vickar, Gillian. 'A Fairly Unconventional Writer.' *Canadian Author and Bookman* 63.2 (1988): 7.

Wertheimer Cast Bronze Sculpture. http://www.ewertheimer.com. Accessed 28 Jan. 2002.

Wiggins, Genevieve. *L.M. Montgomery.* New York: Twayne, 1992.

Index